The Blood-Tinted Waters of the Shenandoah

THE 1864 VALLEY CAMPAIGN'S BATTLE OF COOL SPRING, JULY 17-18, 1864

by Jonathan A. Noyalas

EMERGING CIVIL WAR SERIES

Chris Mackowski, series editor
Cecily Nelson Zander, chief historian

The Emerging Civil War Series

offers compelling, easy-to-read overviews of some of the Civil War's most important battles and stories.

Recipient of the Army Historical Foundation's Lieutenant General Richard G. Trefry Award for contributions to the literature on the history of the U.S. Army

Also part of the Emerging Civil War Series:

Bloody Autumn: The Shenandoah Valley Campaign of 1864 by Daniel T. Davis and Phillip S. Greenwalt

Call Out the Cadets: The Battle of New Market, May 15, 1864 by Sarah Kay Bierle

Determined to Stand and Fight: The Battle of Monocacy, July 9, 1864 by Ryan T. Quint

Grant's Left Hook: The Bermuda Hundred Campaign, May 5–June 7, 1864 by Sean Michael Chick

Hurricane from the Heavens: The Battle of Cold Harbor, May 26–June 5, 1864 by Daniel T. Davis and Phillip S. Greenwalt

John Brown's Raid: Harpers Ferry and the Coming of the Civil War, October 16–18, 1859 by Jon-Erik M. Gilot and Kevin R. Pawlak

The Most Desperate Acts of Gallantry: George A. Custer in the Civil War by Daniel T. Davis

Also by Jonathan A. Noyalas:

Slavery and Freedom in the Shenandoah Valley during the Civil War Era (University Press of Florida, 2021)

Civil War Legacy in the Shenandoah: Remembrance, Reunion & Reconciliation (The History Press, 2015)

The Battle of Fisher's Hill: Breaking the Shenandoah Valley's Gibraltar (The History Press, 2013)

The Battle of Cedar Creek: Victory from the Jaws of Defeat (The History Press, 2009)

For a complete list of titles in the Emerging Civil War Series, visit www.emergingcivilwar.com.

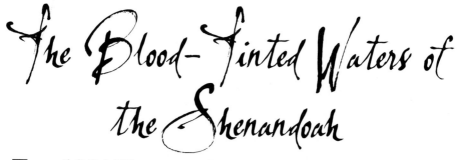

The Blood-Tinted Waters of the Shenandoah

THE 1864 VALLEY CAMPAIGN'S BATTLE OF COOL SPRING, JULY 17-18, 1864

by Jonathan A. Noyalas

EMERGING CIVIL WAR SERIES

SB

Savas Beatie

California

First edition, first printing

ISBN-13: 978-161121-715-5 (paperback)
ISBN-13: 978-161121-716-2 (ebook)

Library of Congress Control Number: 2024009807

Names: Noyalas, Jonathan A., author.
Title: The Blood-Tinted Waters of the Shenandoah: The 1864 Valley
Campaign's Battle of Cool Spring, July 17–18, 1864 / by Jonathan A. Noyalas.
Description: El Dorado Hills, CA : Savas Beatie, [2024] | Series: Emerging Civil
War series | Summary: "This book examines Gen. Horatio Wright's pursuit of
Gen. Jubal Early into the Shenandoah and the clash on July 17–18, 1864. It
analyzes the decisions of leaders on both sides, explores the environment's impact on
the battle, and investigates how the combat impacted the soldiers and their families in
its immediate aftermath and for decades thereafter"-- Provided by publisher.
Identifiers: LCCN 2024009807 | ISBN 9781611217155 (paperback) | ISBN
9781611217162 (ebook)
Subjects: LCSH: Cool Spring, Battle of, Va., 1864. | Wright, Horatio Gouverneur,
1820-1899--Military leadership. | Early, Jubal Anderson, 1816-1894--Military
leadership.
Classification: LCC E476.66 .N69 2024 | DDC 973.7/37--dc23/eng/20240229
LC record available at https://lccn.loc.gov/2024009807

SB

Published by
Savas Beatie LLC
989 Governor Drive, Suite 102
El Dorado Hills, California 95762
916-941-6896
sales@savasbeatie.com
www.savasbeatie.com

Savas Beatie titles are available at special discounts for bulk purchases in the United States by corporations, institutions, and other organizations. For more details, e-mail us at sales@savasbeatie.com or visit our website at www.savasbeatie.com for additional information.

Printed and bound in the United Kingdom

Dedicated to the memory of Mike Smith,
a wonderful friend and supporter of Shenandoah University's
McCormick Civil War Institute's efforts at Cool Spring.
May he rest in peace.

Table of Contents

Footnotes for this volume are available at
https://emergingcivilwar.com/publication/footnotes/

List of Maps

Maps by Edward Alexander

PHOTO CREDITS: John Russell Bartlett, *Memoirs of Rhode Island Officers Who were Engaged in the Service of Their Country during the Great Rebellion of the South* (jrb); *Battles & Leaders of the Civil War* (bl); William Beavans Diary and Letters, Southern Historical Collection, Wilson Library, The University of North Carolina at Chapel Hill (unc); Samuel Clarke Farrar, *The Twenty-Second Pennsylvania Cavalry and the Ringgold Battalion, 1861-1865* (scf); Jon-Erik Gilot (jeg); Library of Congress (loc); Charles H. Lynch, *The Civil War Diary of Charles H. Lynch, 18th Connecticut Volunteers* (cl); Walter Clark, *Histories of the Several Regiments and Battalions from North Carolina* (wcnc); Francis Trevelyan Miller, *The Photographic History of the Civil War* (phcw); John T. Nagle, *An Appeal to President Roosevelt for Justice to a Class of Acting Assistant Surgeons of the United States Army Who Served in the Civil War* (jtn); National Archives (na); George W. Nichols, A *Soldier's Story of His Regiment* (gwn); Jonathan A. Noyalas (jn); Nicholas P. Picerno private collection (np); Shenandoah University's McCormick Civil War Institute (mcwi); Dana B. Shoaf private collection (dbs); Mike Smith private collection (ms); Edmund C. Stedman and Ellen M. Hutchinson, eds., *A Library of American Literature: From the Earliest Settlement to the Present Time*, Volume 11 (al); Henry M. Tower, *Historical Sketches Relating to Spencer, Mass.* (hs); United States Army Heritage and Education Center, Carlisle, PA (ahec); Richard A. Wolfe private collection (rw)

For the Emerging Civil War Series

Theodore P. Savas, *publisher*

Sarah Keeney, *editorial consultant*

Veronica Kane, *production supervisor*

David Snyder, *copyeditor*

Nancy Hale, *proofreader*

Chris Mackowski, *series editor and co-founder*

Cecily Nelson Zander, *chief historian*

Kristopher D. White, *emeritus editor*

Layout by Jess Maxfield

Maps by Edward Alexander

Acknowledgments

Writing a book is never the work of a solitary individual. I wish to take this opportunity to express my deepest gratitude to the following individuals who have assisted with this project: Edward Alexander, for crafting excellent maps; Dr. Jeff Coker, dean of the College of Arts & Sciences, for his support of this project and all of the McCormick Civil War Institute's efforts at Cool Spring; Dr. Tracy Fitzsimmons, president of Shenandoah University, for her support of this book and the McCormick Civil War Institute's myriad projects; Jon-Erik Gilot, friend and fellow historian, for his scholarship on the 170th Ohio and for providing the photograph of Col. Joseph Thoburn's tombstone; Brian Matthew Jordan, a wonderful friend and constant supporter, for writing the foreword; Chris Mackowski, a fine historian and fellow fan of the Buffalo Bills for his support of this project; Nicholas Picerno, a great friend, fine historian, and champion of battlefield preservation in the Shenandoah Valley, for allowing access to items in his personal collection; Shenandoah University's Library staff for always being willing to

assist, particularly with interlibrary loan requests; Ted Savas, publisher of this book and so many important titles in Civil War history; Dana B. Shoaf, a longtime friend, former editor of *Civil War Times*, and currently director of interpretation at the National Museum of Civil War Medicine for permitting use of the image of Elijah Massey; Jonathan E. Tracey, a good friend and fine public historian, for contributing an essay for this volume's appendix on Col. Joseph Thoburn; and Richard A. Wolfe for the use of the image of Lt. Col. Thomas Morris.

Finally, my loving and supportive wife, Brandy, and wonderful son, Alex, deserve special recognition. They are the motivation for all that I do and as with all book projects have supported me in numerous ways.

The peaceful waters of the Shenandoah River today present a stark contrast to the carnage experienced along its banks during the battle of Cool Spring. (jn)

Foreword

BY BRIAN MATTHEW JORDAN

Even the most diligent students of the Civil War's military history might be hard pressed to identify the battle of Cool Spring, a sprite, sanguinary clash that unfolded along the banks of the Shenandoah River in Clarke County, Virginia, on July 18, 1864. On that day, elements of two federal army corps met up with rebel general Jubal A. Early's Army of the Valley as it slinked back up the Shenandoah, nursing the regrets of a failed foray to Washington, D.C. Fought during a brutal summer whose surreal scenes—the fires of the Wilderness, the fury of the Mule Shoe, the frontal assaults at Cold Harbor—overwhelmed even those well acquainted with the war's devastations, the engagement at Cool Spring was quickly eclipsed in national memory. As federal troops trundled into the works around Petersburg and battled their way ever closer to Atlanta, the press and the lay public had reason to shift their sights far from Island Ford.

This book, then, is an act of historical recovery—skillfully narrating the details of a battle that many histories have misplaced. But it is substantially more,

View of the Shenandoah River looking south from atop the bluffs where Union batteries were posted on July 18, 1864. (jn)

because historian Jonathan A. Noyalas, the dean of the Civil War in the Shenandoah Valley, has rendered exquisitely legible the gap that yawns between messy human experiences and tidy historical narratives. Soldiers (and, by extension, their families and communities back home, who also fight) assign weight and meaning to battles in ways that do not always align with the subsequent assessments of starched historians. Indeed, events that barely register on our rubrics of significance loomed large in the lives of ordinary soldiers. The grief of widowhood was felt no less acutely because a husband was felled in a skirmish. Slugs of lead proved no less deadly in brief actions. Physical and psychological injuries were not the exclusive province of headline-seizing battles; the quiet agonies of veteranhood visited the survivors of engagements large and small.

Each summer Shenandoah University's McCormick Civil War Institute conducts a camp for children at Cool Spring. Among the topics explored are camp life and the everyday experiences of soldiers. (jn)

Historians routinely consider the significance of a battle by evaluating its operational results, strategic consequences, or political implications. Noyalas's metric is much simpler and, I submit, more humane. He argues that Cool Spring was a significant battle not because it changed the course or outcome of a military campaign, but because it changed the lives of those who fought there. Noyalas's approach urges us to reconsider not just our Civil War past, but what we deem significant about it. The war was comprised of many similar actions that have scarcely merited the attention of historians. Even so, these engagements consumed the lives of their contemporaries—men and women, of course, who could never be certain how the war would turn out. The war was punctuated with contingencies and close-run things; it brimmed with lost alternatives and moments of futility. Those experiences, no less than Shiloh and Gettysburg, are part of the Civil War fabric.

Noyalas's relentlessly human account of Cool Spring takes inventory of combat's lived costs. In these pages, for instance, we meet the soldier from Killingly, Connecticut, who returned to the battlefield to comb for his dead brother's remains—consumed by a survivor's guilt as profound as his personal grief. Noyalas demonstrates that no tactical map can adequately record the totality of what happened on a Civil War battlefield, for the consequences of combat rippled out in both time and space, annexing lives, families, and communities—sometimes for generations. Noyalas captures that complex dynamic by punctuating his battle narrative with telling vignettes—many drawn from pension files, service records, and civilian newspapers—tracing what I have called elsewhere the "human longitude" of war. A stubborn hour defending a nameless ridge could truly endure for fifty or more years. In Noyalas's account, the human consequences of battle are not siloed into a final chapter; rather, they are seamlessly integrated into the narrative of the battle itself. With this short volume, Noyalas supplies both a template for future writers and a keen reminder that Civil War battles are rich laboratories in which to observe the human experience in all its complexity.

Happily, readers interested in Cool Spring are not limited to this handsome volume. Together with his troop of talented undergraduate students at the McCormick Civil War Institute, Jonathan Noyalas has brought this battlefield—a significant portion of which is now owned by Shenandoah University—to new interpretive life. Exploiting the latest technologies, Noyalas and his students have developed not only a walking tour and exhibits, but also an augmented reality experience that harmonizes with the arguments you will soon encounter. I have had the privilege to walk the battlefield with Jonathan, and I can only hope that many others, inspired by the words that follow, will choose to visit this moving site. Study what happened on July 18, 1864, but, more importantly, reflect on what Civil War stories we choose to tell— and whose Civil War histories we choose to write.

BRIAN MATTHEW JORDAN *is associate professor of history and chair of the history department at Sam Houston State University and author of* Marching Home: Union Veterans and Their Unending Civil War, *a Pulitzer Prize finalist.*

"As seen by the men in the ranks, it was strange that a small force was ordered over that river to cope with Early's force, and the 6th Corps near by. . . . Some things are hard to understand in the life of a soldier."

—*Corporal Charles Lynch*
18th Connecticut Infantry

Prologue

Scores of Union soldiers wounded during the battle of Cool Spring on July 18, 1864, aided by comrades who helped them navigate their way from the battlefield on the Shenandoah River's western shore to the immediate safety of the Shenandoah's eastern side, inspired poet Edith Thomas. A native of Ohio who enjoyed a successful career as a poet and editor for Century Dictionary and Harper's magazine, with no discernable connections to the battle, Thomas authored "A Christopher of the Shenandoah, Island Ford, Snickers Gap, July 18, 1864," approximately two decades after what proved to be the bloodiest battle fought in Clarke County, Virginia, during the Civil War. What motivated Thomas to author the ten-stanza poem from the perspective of a solitary Union soldier, "the Orderly," is unclear.

Throughout the poem—which appears in this volume's appendix—"the Orderly," at great personal risk, attempted all humanly possible to rescue his comrades utilizing "a battered and oarless barge."

Sycamore tree along the Shenandoah River's eastern shore believed, according to oral histories, to be a hideout for freedom seekers. (jn)

Efforts to carry wounded Union soldiers across the Shenandoah River from the battlefield's western shore to its eastern side indeed occurred; however, no such incident as Thomas's poem depicted transpired. Nonetheless, "A Christopher of the Shenandoah" exemplified the American soldier's commitment to never leave a comrade behind on the battlefield. For decades, well into the twentieth century, "A Christopher of the Shenandoah" proved a staple at Memorial Day ceremonies from coast to coast.

Unfortunately, Thomas's poem, much like the fighting that took place along the banks of the

Shenandoah River on July 18, 1864, fell into obscurity. While the battle of Cool Spring, the result of the Union pursuit of Confederate general Jubal A. Early's Army of the Valley following Early's push to the gates of Washington in mid-July 1864, pales in comparison to engagements such as Shiloh, Antietam, Chickamauga, or Gettysburg, it offers a critical reminder that the litmus test for a battle's meaning should never be confined to the number of troops engaged, amount of casualties, strategic consequences, or political gains. For the wife transformed into a widow, to the child made an orphan, to a soldier wounded in combat, or veteran traumatized

View of the Shenandoah River from its eastern side. On the night of July 18, 1864, many Union soldiers, not just one as poet Edith Thomas imagined in her poem, helped evacuate wounded Union soldiers from the Shenandoah River's western bank to its eastern shore. (jn)

Confederate veteran John Alexander Stikeleather was forever haunted by what happened at Cool Spring. (wcnc)

by what occurred on the battlefield, an engagement's significance was defined by how that battle forever altered their earthly existence.

Nearly 15,000 troops fought along the Shenandoah River's banks on July 17-18, 1864. Approximately 1,000 soldiers became casualties. While neither Union or Confederate soldiers possessed delusions about the battle being among the conflict's most significant engagements, to soldiers such as the 4th North Carolina's John Alexander Stikeleather, who watched his friend Martin Snow die "in ten seconds" after being shot in the neck and was haunted by that moment for the remainder of his life, or the 18th Connecticut's Pvt. Samuel Smith, who saw a Confederate bullet strike his brother James and watched helplessly as the Shenandoah River's current swept James away to his grave, the battle of Cool Spring proved the war's most significant battle.

For Nancy DeArmond, wife of the 30th North Carolina's Sgt. Aaron Leonidas DeArmond, who died from wounds received during the battle, the battle of Cool Spring thrust her into widowhood with the immense responsibility of now caring for four fatherless children.

Four-year-old Mary Ellen Farley never really had an opportunity to get to know her father, Pvt. Joshua Farley. Farley is buried in the Winchester National Cemetery, grave 709. (jn)

When a Confederate bullet killed the 116th Ohio's Pvt. Joshua Farley his four-year-old daughter Mary Ellen, whose mother died in 1862, became an orphan.

Lieutenant Ransom Griffin, one of Farley's comrades, assumed guardianship of Mary Ellen.

During the final thirty-four years of his life Col. James Washburn, shot through the left eye while leading the 116th Ohio Infantry to bolster Col. Joseph Thoburn's northern flank, received frequent reminders of Cool Spring's consequences each time he looked into the mirror and viewed the disfigured face staring back.

To the aforementioned soldiers and civilians, the "sharp and bloody engagement . . . on the Shenandoah" proved a life-altering moment.

"We've Scared Abe Lincoln Like Hell"

CHAPTER ONE
JULY 9–12, 1864

The residents of Washington, D.C., tried to maintain a sense of routine during the second week of July 1864. Stone masons worked on the north face of the United States Patent Office, shopkeepers went about their daily tasks of stocking shelves and selling wares, construction crews repaired pavements throughout the city, and children played in the streets. To the casual observer, all appeared, as Lois Bryan Adams, an employee at the United States Department of Agriculture, recorded in her diary, that "business seems progressing about the same as before . . . happily oblivious."

All, however, was not normal. Following the victory of Lt. Gen. Jubal Early's Confederate force at the battle of Monocacy on July 9, 1864, streams of refugees poured into the nation's capital and the city's inhabitants prepared for a possible attack. Rumors circulated wildly about the strength of Early's command and his next target. Horatio Nelson Taft, an examiner at the United States Patent Office, wrote

Union artillery at Cool Spring during the battle's 155th anniversary commemoration in 2018. (jn)

As Lt. Gen. Jubal Early's Confederates neared Washington, D.C., during the second week of July 1864, apprehensions among the capital city's inhabitants grew significantly. (loc)

General Robert E. Lee hoped that sending Early to the Shenandoah Valley in 1864 would yield the same results as Stonewall Jackson's successes there two years earlier. (loc)

in his diary on July 9: "The rebel force is estimated at all numbers from five thousand to twenty thousand. . . . It is supposed that they will make an attempt upon this city or Baltimore next."

While speculation about the strength or intentions of Early's army ran rampant, most seemed to comprehend the purpose of his mission—to create a strategic diversion and therefore hinder Lt. Gen. Ulysses S. Grant's campaign to take Richmond. One Washingtonian concluded correctly on July 9 that "this rebel 'raid' is supposed to be intended to draw Grant away from Richmond to defend Washington."

All doubts as to Early's intended target ceased in the early afternoon of July 11, 1864, as his command stood north of Washington in front of Fort Stevens. News of approximately 10,000 Confederates situated on the capital's outskirts, coupled with artillery fire, shook some of the capital's inhabitants to the core as the war had now come to their doorstep. Lois Bryan Adams, unnerved by the "considerable cannonading," wrote of this sobering reality: "We know that 'the front' now is no mythical or distant place far down the Rapidan, the Rappahannock, or the James; but, for the present at least, a reality terribly near."

The fear that Adams and other Washingtonians felt that second week of July stemmed from a scheme Confederate war planners had developed one month earlier to alleviate mounting pressure on the Confederate capital by sending Early's Second Corps, Army of Northern Virginia, to the Shenandoah Valley to create a strategic diversion and, if possible, threaten Washington. Two years earlier, in the spring of 1862, when Maj. Gen. George B. McClellan's Army of the Potomac approached the gates of Richmond, Confederate general Thomas J. "Stonewall" Jackson's army carried out a campaign of diversion in the Shenandoah Valley. Jackson's victories contributed significantly to Richmond's security and buoyed the Confederacy's spirit mightily. If Early could replicate Jackson's success, the threats to Richmond could once again dissipate.

While the departure of Early's corps from the Army of Northern Virginia came with risks, most notably diminishing the army's strength as Union forces concentrated south of Petersburg, the Army of

Northern Virginia's commander, Gen. Robert E. Lee, recognized the benefits of utilizing the Shenandoah Valley as a diversionary theater of war. "I acknowledge the advantage of expelling the enemy from the Valley. The only difficulty is the means. It would [take] one corps of this army" and might "hazard the defense of Richmond," Lee explained to President Jefferson Davis on June 11. While indeed precarious, with all weighed in the balance, Lee believed sending Early to the Shenandoah Valley "the best" decision "that can be made."

When Lee met with Early on June 12, 1864, Lee explained all he hoped Early's campaign would achieve. First, Lee wanted Early to defeat Union general David Hunter and drive him from Lynchburg, Virginia, a vital transportation and logistical hub. Throughout the spring of 1864, Hunter menaced the Confederacy's efforts in the Shenandoah. Hunter defeated Brig. Gen. William "Grumble" Jones's Confederates at Piedmont on June 5, cleared the Shenandoah Valley of Confederates, occupied the strategically significant city of Staunton in the Valley's southern end, and destroyed property Hunter deemed important to the Confederacy's cause, including homes believed to be utilized as safe havens for Confederate irregulars, the Virginia Military Institute, and railroads.

An 1822 graduate of West Point, Maj. Gen. David Hunter's inability to defend Lynchburg, Virginia, created an opportunity for Early's Confederates to march to the outskirts of the nation's capital. (loc)

Shortly after 3:00 a.m. on June 13, Early's Second Corps departed from the vicinity of Gaines's Mill and headed west. Early's command arrived in Lynchburg on the afternoon of June 17. By the following day, Early's command forced Hunter from Lynchburg. With Hunter defeated and moving deep into West Virginia, Early focused on that part of Lee's instructions that instructed the Second Corps "to move down the Valley, cross the Potomac near Leesburg in Loudoun County, or at or above Harper's Ferry . . . and threaten Washington City."

Early's army moved rapidly through the Shenandoah Valley. By July 4 Early's army reached Harpers Ferry. Five days later, Early's command engaged and defeated Maj. Gen. Lew Wallace's force at the battle of Monocacy. On July 11, Early's command reached present-day Silver Spring, Maryland, located north of Washington. As some in Early's ranks peered at Washington, they "could see the church steeples and

Although tactically defeated at Monocacy, Maj. Gen. Lew Wallace's efforts there bought valuable time to better prepare for Washington's defense. Sixteen years after the battle, Wallace published *Ben-Hur*. (loc)

Private George Nichols, 61st Georgia Infantry, was among the soldiers in Early's army who hoped they would occupy Washington and capture President Abraham Lincoln. (gwn)

Scene of the fight in front of Fort Stevens. Although Early did not attempt to capture the nation's capital, the presence of Confederate troops heightened anxieties among Washington's defenders and its inhabitants. (loc)

dome of the capitol building, and could hear the city clocks strike" and wanted to attack. Private George Nichols, 61st Georgia Infantry, wrote enthusiastically that "we privates wanted to charge and take the city, and we wanted to capture 'Uncle Abe.'"

As Early surveyed the area around Fort Stevens—a fortification located north of the capital which protected the Seventh Street Road, an avenue described by one chronicler as "the vital artery . . . leading directly into Washington from Silver Spring"—shortly after noon on July 11, he "discovered that the works were but feebly manned." Sensing opportunity, Early summoned Maj. Gen. Robert Rodes to "immediately" maneuver his division "into line as rapidly as possible, throw out skirmishers, and move into the works if he could."

Although it seemed simple enough, Rodes's command, along with all of Early's men, were exhausted. Over the course of the past month, Early's regiments had marched nearly 500 miles, fought multiple engagements, and contended with extreme heat. Confederate soldier John Worsham captured the toll all of this had taken on Early's command: "We had marched during that time four hundred and sixty-nine miles, fought several combats, and one battle . . . many of them were physically unable to keep up." Early admitted on July 14 in his report to Lee that "the men were almost completely exhausted and not in a condition to make an attack." Simply put, "the spirit

Interior view of Fort Stevens. Originally named Fort Massachusetts, the fort's name was changed to honor Brig. Gen. Isaac Stevens who was killed on September 1, 1862, at the battle of Chantilly. (loc)

was willing," as historian Benjamin Franklin Cooling concluded, "but the bodies were not."

As Rodes attempted to bring his men into position, Early spied "a cloud of dust in the rear of the works towards Washington." Early reckoned this to be the arrival of Union reinforcements. That perception, coupled with Union batteries opening fire on Early's army, dashed any expectations for a Confederate attack. "This defeated our hopes of getting possession of the works by surprise," Early explained. While Early's command exchanged shots with the defenders of Fort Stevens, Early abandoned all ideas of an assault.

In retrospect, some Confederates believed this a prudent decision. As a Virginia soldier in Early's command surveyed Fort Stevens and the surrounding area on July 11, it appeared "the most formidable" fortification he "ever saw." Confederate John Worsham noted that "trees had been cut down" in front of Fort Stevens "so that the limbs pointed towards us and they were sharpened . . . The enemy had a full sweep of the ground for at least a mile in their front." Worsham candidly stated that Early's "force would not be able to take them."

Once Early decided he would not strike, he next determined how long he should stay. Early reasoned that the longer his corps remained, the greater chance his command confronted of being cut off and destroyed. Aware that the "loss" of his "force would have . . . such a depressing effect upon the country"

Major General Robert Rodes was regarded as one of the best division commanders in the Army of Northern Virginia. Following his death at the Third Battle of Winchester, September 19, 1864, the *Richmond Dispatch* characterized Rodes "as one of the most brave and gallant spirits." (bl)

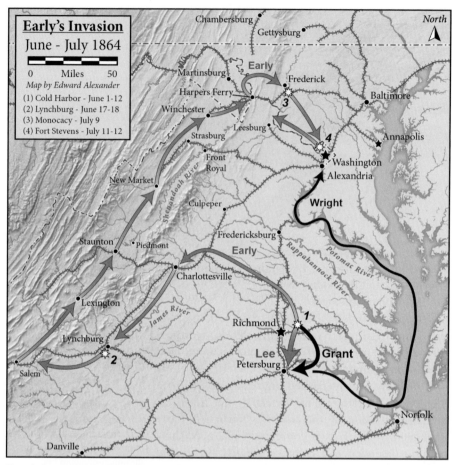

EARLY'S INVASION, JUNE-JULY 1864—As Early's army moved north through the Shenandoah Valley en route to Washington in the summer of 1864, newspapers in the North pondered what Early hoped to achieve. A correspondent for the *Chicago Times* wrote on July 7: "It is impossible . . . to arrive at any definite conclusion in regard to the objects of the movement of the Confederate forces into Maryland."

and prove a "fatal disaster" to the Confederate war effort, Early decided to withdraw during the night of July 12.

As Early's columns departed, those in the ranks assessed the significance of their movement to Washington's gates. Although the Confederates had not attacked, Early's presence forced Lt. Gen. Ulysses S. Grant to send troops from the VI and XIX Corps to Washington. Those troops began to arrive in the nation's capital around 2:00 p.m. on July 11. Father James Sheeran, a chaplain in the 14th Louisiana Infantry, viewed the campaign as a success. "The object of his [Early's] mission was accomplished; to

draw their [Union] forces from Richmond," Sheeran wrote in his diary. The 5th Alabama's Henry Beck agreed with Sheeran's assessment. Although Beck admitted he and his comrades "were disappointed" they did not attack, he concluded that "our object in this expedition no doubt was accomplished, by withdrawing" Union forces "from Richmond." Lieutenant Colonel Alexander Swift "Sandie" Pendleton, a member of Early's staff, thought the army's push to Fort Stevens not only strategically significant, but a remarkably well-managed effort that prevented significant losses, save those who fell victim to the heat. Pendleton explained that while some might brand Early's inability to take Washington a "failure," it was "necessary to call to mind the fearful heat" and that Early "was undoubtedly prudent to withdraw. I think it showed good management to come off so well." Not all viewed the movement to Washington's gates so positively. Private Caleb Linker, 57th North Carolina Infantry, believed Early's army accomplished nothing. Decades after the conflict, one of Early's division commanders, Maj. Gen. John B. Gordon, recognized that while the Second Corps "succeeded in" getting "General Grant to detach a portion of his army from Lee's front at Petersburg," Early missed an opportunity. Gordon thought Early "undoubtedly could have marched on Washington."

Confederate soldiers wounded during the fighting in the Shenandoah Valley in the autumn of 1864 and recuperating at a hospital in Americus, Georgia, also thought Early should have attacked. Nurse Kate Cummings overheard some "wounded men,

Although Early's army did not attack the nation's capital, the presence of it compelled Ulysses S. Grant (left) to send reinforcements to Washington—troops that Grant could have used to further pressure the Army of Northern Virginia at Petersburg. (loc)

Lieutenant Colonel Alexander Swift "Sandie" Pendleton (center) was among those in Early's army who believed the Confederate advance to Washington's outskirts strategically benefitted the Confederate war effort in Virginia. (loc)

Major General John B. Gordon (right) criticized Early's generalship in 1864 and believed Early could have attacked Washington. (loc)

Confederates outside of Early's army, including Brig. Gen. Edward Porter Alexander, chief of artillery for the Army of Northern Virginia's First Corps, believed Early's advance to Washington provided the Confederacy with some strategic benefits. (loc)

who were with General Early in his late disastrous campaign . . . blame General Early for not marching right up to Washington, as they think he could have taken it." North Carolinian John Alexander Stikeleather had little doubt that Early's army could attack and capture Washington. However, he did not believe Early's army strong enough to maintain control. Stikeleather surmised that "had we taken Washington, the advantages to us perhaps, would have been temporary."

As news of Early's advance to Washington and subsequent withdrawal spread throughout the Confederacy, soldiers and civilians alike offered their perspectives about what, if anything, Early's campaign achieved. Brigadier General Edward Porter Alexander, the chief of artillery for the Army of Northern Virginia's First Corps, thought it "absurd" that Early could have captured Washington. Although Alexander recognized that Early's movement deprived Grant of "those two corps [VI and XIX]," he thought that the prospect of Early achieving anything beyond a strategic diversion "purely bluff." Believing that "Grant . . . was not easily bluffed," Alexander thought Early's corps could have served the Confederate war effort better had it been sent to reinforce Gen. Joseph E. Johnston's command near Atlanta, Georgia.

Confederate civilians, such as Mary Greenhow Lee, did not debate the strategic implications of Early's movements, but rather focused on how it buoyed morale. Lee, one of the staunchest Confederate women in Winchester, Virginia, believed Early's campaign marked "a glorious era in our national history." Lucy Buck, a Confederate resident of Front Royal, did not hold such a joyous perspective. When Buck learned that Early had withdrawn from Washington's gates and pulled back across the Potomac into Virginia, she pondered in her diary on July 16 "what it all means." While Buck expressed faith in Early, the decision to withdraw without launching an assault made little sense to her. "General Early has an object in it, no doubt, and fully understands all he intends to do. Wish I did too," Buck wrote.

In his report to Lee, written two days after the withdrawal, Early appeared apologetic that he could not capture Washington. "I am sorry I did not succeed in capturing Washington," Early explained to his superior. Nonetheless, Early had carried out Lee's directive to "threaten Washington city" and pull troops away from Grant. On the night of July 12, in a conversation with one of his staff officers, Maj. Henry Kyd Douglas, Early shared his perspective about what he believed the advance to Washington achieved. "In his falsetto drawl," Early crowed to Douglas that "we haven't taken Washington, but we've scared Abe Lincoln like h[ell]!"

While true that he did not capture Washington, Early's boast about how the Confederate advance to the capital's northern periphery impacted President Lincoln proved erroneous.

As much as President Abraham Lincoln might have wanted to order an immediate pursuit of Early's command, he refused to do so as he believed Grant would develop a suitable plan. (loc)

"The March Is a Rather Severe One"

CHAPTER TWO
JULY 13–16, 1864

The peacefulness of the Retreat along the banks of the Shenandoah River would be shattered as Union Forces pursued Early's army into the Shenandoah Valley. (jn)

While Early's advance to the national capital's outskirts certainly heightened fears among many Washingtonians, President Lincoln, despite Early's boast that he "scared Lincoln like he[ll]," remained, at least in the estimation of those closest to him, unruffled. Possessed by the utmost confidence in the fortifications that surrounded the capital, Lincoln, while vigilant, did not believe Early capable of seizing Washington. According to John Hay, Lincoln's private secretary, on July 11: "The President is in good feather this evening. He seems not in the least concerned about the safety of Washington." On that day, and once Lincoln learned of Early's withdrawal, the chief executive's primary "concern," as Hay recalled, "seems to be whether we can bag or destroy" Early's command. On the morning of July 13, Lincoln received reports "that the enemy is retiring from every point." Lincoln and many in Washington appeared "eager for the pursuit to begin." John Hay recalled that once Lincoln received confirmation of Early's retreat, Lincoln thought "we should push our whole column . . . & cut off as many as possible of the retreating raiders."

President Abraham Lincoln, with his two secretaries John Nicolay (seated) and John Hay (standing). Hay did not believe Early's advance to Washington's outskirts "scared Abe Lincoln like h[ell]!" (loc)

As much as Lincoln might have wanted an immediate pursuit, he would not order it. When he first met with Ulysses S. Grant in early 1864, Lincoln informed Grant "that he had never professed to be a military man or to know how campaigns should be conducted." While Lincoln acknowledged his lack of military ability, he did inform the new general in chief that so long as a commander did not procrastinate, Lincoln would not intervene. Lincoln explained to Grant that he "never wanted to interfere" in military campaigns. The president's private secretaries, John Nicolay and John Hay, explained that "the President, true to the position he had taken when Grant was made general-in-chief, would not interfere." Nonetheless, as Early slipped away, Lincoln felt much "anguish." So too did some of Washington's residents. "Union people here will be terribly exasperated if they are allowed to escape," Lois Adams groaned.

Although Lincoln believed it a simple task to "cut off" Early's corps, the charge, at least in the estimation of Assistant Secretary of War Charles Dana, proved nearly impossible. "The idea of cutting off their retreat would seem to be futile, for there are plenty of fords and ferries now in their control where they can cross the Potomac and get off, in spite of our efforts to intercept them," Dana concluded. At 11:30 a.m. on July 12, unaware that Early would withdraw that night, Dana telegraphed Grant at City Point and identified another problem: no one officer exerted control over all of the United States troops assembled in the area. "Nothing can be done here toward pursuing or cutting off the enemy for want of a commander. . . . [T]here is no head to the whole," Dana complained. Dana believed that nothing would happen until Grant appointed one. Additionally, Dana and Secretary of War Edwin Stanton urged Grant to be explicit in his orders. Stanton and Dana did not want "advice or suggestions." Secretary Dana worried that until Grant directed "positively and explicitly what is to be done, everything will go on in the [same] deplorable and fatal way." Grant agreed.

Assistant Secretary of War Charles Dana believed there were many challenges in pursuing Early. (loc)

Among all of the officers in Washington, Grant believed Maj. Gen. Horatio Wright, commander of the VI Corps, best suited to command the pursuit force. Grant wrote Maj. Gen. Henry Halleck, chief of staff, late on July 12: "Give orders assigning Maj. Gen. H. G. Wright to supreme command of all troops moving out against the enemy, regardless of the rank of other commanders." Grant urged Wright to gather as many troops as "he possibly can" and "push Early to the last moment."

Despite Grant's belief that "Wright is the man" to drive "the enemy out of Maryland in confusion" some, including Halleck, possessed doubts. Halleck did not necessarily doubt Wright's ability to command, but the chief of staff harbored reservations about how effective Wright could be with approximately 10,000 troops. Despite the reality that Early's and Wright's commands possessed nearly the same number of troops, Halleck estimated Early's command "at 23,000-25,000, exclusive of cavalry." Assistant Secretary Dana received similar appraisals of Early's strength. "The force of the enemy is everywhere stated at from 20,000 to 30,000," Dana informed Grant. Reports in newspapers also inflated the size of Early's command. A Baltimore journalist estimated Early's overall strength at 45,000 and claimed that

Major General Horatio Wright (left), commander of the Union force that pursued Early, graduated from West Point in 1841. He ranked second in his class. Wright enjoyed a distinguished career in the army until his retirement in 1884. After he became the army's chief engineer in 1879, he managed the completion of the Washington Monument. (loc)

Vermonter Aldace Walker (center) harbored concerns about the ability of Union forces to defeat Early. (np)

Nicknamed "Old Brains," Maj. Gen. Henry Halleck (right) graduated from West Point in 1839. Halleck ranked third in his class. In the years before the Civil War, Halleck wrote much about defense, including *Elements of Military Art and Science*. (loc)

reinforcements from General James Longstreet's corps were en route to support Early. Although none of this was true, perception was reality, and it cultivated uncertainty. On July 13, Halleck explained to Grant that while he believed "Wright could attack Early's rear," the chief of staff thought Wright's force "too weak to attack [the] main force."

Wright's command departed the nation's capital on the afternoon of July 13. Initially the column moved at a snail's pace. Captain Aldace Walker, 11th Vermont Infantry, wrote to his father that the pursuit force "tried to get away by 3 p.m., but could only move by inches." By 9:00 p.m., Walker estimated Wright's force marched only three miles. Various factors, including insufferable heat and a wagon train of "new mules and green drivers" that "began to break down," helped account for the slow start. A veteran in the 37th Massachusetts Infantry branded the "green" teamsters "self-important, lazy, worthless fellows almost without exception." Plagued by this incompetent wagon train, Wright complained to Halleck: "The march is a rather severe one, the men straggling badly. The teams are green, and the trains consequently move much less rapidly than the infantry."

Undeterred, Wright's command picked up the pace significantly and marched through the night in an attempt to gain some ground on Early. By 7:00 a.m., Wright's troops covered approximately twenty miles. Wright, aware that his veterans "had nary a mouthful to eat," halted the column that morning and allowed his men to rest for approximately three hours. By late morning, Wright's force resumed the march. Wright's command reached Poolesville, Maryland, during the evening of July 14.

When Wright's command arrived, Early's army, sans a contingent of cavalry protecting its rear, had already crossed the Potomac River into Virginia at White's Ford. A Vermont officer who possessed some hope of intercepting Early's troops lamented to his father from Poolesville, "we were too late." At 6:00 p.m., Wright telegraphed Halleck with the news that "the main body of the enemy, with trains, had crossed." With Early in Virginia, Wright thought it senseless to pursue, particularly because Wright believed Early's force numerically superior. Wright deemed his force "wholly insufficient to justify the following up of the enemy on the other side of the Potomac."

Additionally, Wright's men were exhausted. Despite his command's slow start, Wright's troops had marched approximately thirty miles in the span of twenty-four hours. The distance covered, coupled with the reality that it occurred on "Bad roads and . . . [in] excessive heat," troubled Wright. Marching that distance proved challenging in normal conditions. Temperatures regularly above ninety degrees throughout July's first two weeks, as reported in the nation's capital, coupled with a lack of rain for weeks turned roads into dust. Excessive heat and dusty roads created a dreadful combination for soldiers. Nostrils, throats, and ears filled with dust, while clouds of dust impacted eyesight. As historian Kenneth Noe concluded, "heat and dry weather produced stifling" conditions.

Confederates were not immune from these circumstances, either. Confederate artillerist Henry Robinson Berkeley branded the march from Washington's outskirts to the Potomac as "the most severe" he "ever experienced." The 4th North Carolina Infantry's John Alexander Stikeleather echoed: "Our march from Washington to the south side of the Potomac, was one of extreme fatigue." Major General Stephen Dodson Ramseur, one of Early's division commanders, explained to his wife that "the heat & dust was so great."

The only advantage Early's command possessed was a twenty-four hour head start. This, Wright correctly asserted, "gave" the Confederates "full time to secure his crossing of the river." As Wright weighed

Attorney General Edward Bates was, like so many, infuriated when he learned Early's army crossed the Potomac River. (loc)

the perceived strength of Early's force against the size of his command and the exhausted condition of his troops, he determined it best to "wait" at Poolesville for "instructions" from the War Department as to whether or not he should cross the Potomac and continue the pursuit.

News of Wright's halt incensed President Lincoln. The commander in chief seemed to care little about the distance Wright covered or the conditions in which his command marched. Lincoln wanted Early's army destroyed. On the evening of July 14, Lincoln vented his frustration to John Hay. "Wright telegraphs that he thinks the enemy are all across the Potomac but that he halted . . . for fear he might come across the rebels & catch some of them." Lincoln's words and tone prompted Hay to record in his diary that night: "The Chief is evidently disgusted."

Lincoln was not the only one. Attorney General Edward Bates, who initially possessed "good hope that the invaders will not be allowed to re-cross the Potomac," fumed when he learned Early crossed. "Alas! for the impotence or treachery of our military rulers! Nobody seems disposed to hinder them," Bates wrote in his journal on July 14.

Grant expressed no such frustration. When Grant learned from Assistant Secretary of War Dana that Early escaped across the Potomac, he no longer believed Early's army posed a legitimate threat to the capital. At 8:00 p.m. on July 14 Grant sent a message to Halleck ordering troops from the XIX Corps, initially directed by Grant to join in the pursuit, to be rerouted to City Point. Grant sent another message to Halleck that day which reiterated his desire to return the XIX Corps and also urged Halleck that "The 6th . . . Corps should be got here without any delay." With Early's army back in the Old Dominion, Grant believed Early would march south, up the Valley, and then head east across the Blue Ridge Mountains to strengthen Lee's army at Petersburg. Grant thought it imperative that the two corps reach Petersburg "before the return of the troops sent into the valley by the enemy."

As definitive as he appeared in the opening paragraph of his communique to Halleck on July 14 about returning the VI and XIX Corps to Petersburg, Grant did not desire for the order to be carried out immediately if Wright had an opportunity to weaken Early's force. "I do not intend this as an order to bring Wright back whilst he is in pursuit of the enemy with any prospect of punishing him, but to secure his return at the earliest possible moment after he ceases to be absolutely necessary where he is," Grant explained.

While Grant and Halleck exchanged messages on July 14, Halleck hoped that Maj. Gen. David Hunter, who since his defeat at Lynchburg the previous month finally returned his command to the northern Shenandoah Valley after an arduous journey which coursed through West Virginia, might unite with Wright. Halleck, as he explained to Hunter on July 14, "hoped that this junction might be effected in time to cut off the enemy's passage, or at least to greatly trouble his retreat." Wright too was eager to link with Hunter. At 7:30 p.m. on the 14th Wright sent a message to Hunter from Poolesville: "I am anxious to form a junction with you at the earliest possible moment." The appeals from Halleck and Wright met with no response.

This, coupled with Hunter's lack of communication with war planners in Washington over the previous month, raised Halleck's frustration exponentially. After imploring Hunter to unite with Wright, on the 14th Halleck lambasted Hunter. "You have not answered dispatches, we are left in the dark in regard to your force and movements," Halleck groaned. Halleck's message also made it clear that when Hunter's forces did eventually unite with Wright, that Wright would be in "supreme command of the forces operating on this expedition." So distressed had Halleck become that he closed his communication to Hunter with a recommendation that Brig. Gen. George Crook assume command of those forces from Hunter's Department of West Virginia that would unite with Wright: Hunter's first division commanded by Brig. Gen. Jeremiah Sullivan. Halleck explained to Hunter candidly: "Crook would be a suitable person for the immediate command."

The following day the War Department made Crook's appointment official. "Gen. George Crook is hereby placed in command of all the forces proceeding from this department [of West Virginia] to form a junction with Maj. Gen. H.G. Wright," the order

Lieutenant Colonel Cyrus B. Comstock, a member of Lt. Gen. Ulysses S. Grant's staff, graduated from West Point in 1855. In the war's aftermath, Comstock donated $10,000 to the National Academy of Sciences to establish the Comstock Prize in Physics. The award is given every five years "for researchers in electricity, magnetism, and radiant energy." The first Comstock Prize was awarded in 1913, three years after Comstock's death. (loc)

stated. The news crushed Hunter. Colonel David Hunter Strother, Hunter's cousin and chief of staff, recorded that when the news reached him at Harpers Ferry on the 15th Hunter considered "himself insulted" and "asks to be relieved of command." An enraged Hunter telegraphed President Lincoln on July 17 that Crook's promotion "has entirely destroyed my usefulness." Despite Hunter's earnest "request to be relieved from the command of this department," Lincoln refused to accept Hunter's resignation. Lincoln stated unequivocally to Hunter that Crook's placement in command of the troops that would unite with Wright stemmed not from any deficiencies in Hunter's generalship, but from the belief that "it was thought that you would prefer Crook's commanding your part, to your serving in person under Wright," a general to whom Hunter was superior in rank. "That is all of it. Gen. Grant wishes you to remain in command of the Department, and I do not wish to order otherwise," Lincoln explained.

As Lincoln attempted to calm Hunter, Grant increasingly believed Wright's pursuit senseless. Grant thought that Early no longer presented a threat to the nation's capital. If anything, Grant speculated that Early might, "before returning to Richmond . . . attempt to go through Western Virginia to Ohio possibly taking Pittsburgh by the way." If Early tried to move into western Pennsylvania or Ohio, Grant encouraged those state governments "to have their citizens organized for a sudden emergency." Grant believed that "the great number of discharged [United States] veterans" in these states could be summoned to repel "invasion" or at least "check" it. If Early attempted another push against Washington, Grant hoped the troops in Hunter's Department of West Virginia would be sufficient to "check an invasion until reinforcements" could arrive from Petersburg.

Halleck vehemently disagreed with the general in chief's assessment. "Old Brains" speculated that as soon as Wright's VI Corps departed for Petersburg, "the enemy may come back." Lieutenant Colonel Cyrus B. Comstock, a member of Grant's staff, who journeyed to Washington to convey Grant's strategic vision to Halleck, sent a telegraph to Grant at 10:30 p.m. on July 15 explaining that Halleck would not return Wright until he received "positive orders." Over the next few days Grant and Halleck continued to communicate, but the precise clarity Halleck desired before he sent troops back to Petersburg appeared in none of Grant's messages. For example, on July 16 Grant expressed his desire to return the VI and XIX Corps "if possible."

As the back and forth between Halleck and Grant continued, Wright's command crossed the Potomac River on July 16. A small contingent of Early's troops attempted to contest the crossing, but "a short and vigorous shelling" from Wright's batteries compelled, as Pvt. Wilbur Fisk recalled, the Confederates to "skedaddle . . . out of our way." With Confederates no longer looming on the Potomac's western bank the crossing proved less taxing. Incessant heat and the absence of rain for weeks made the Potomac easily fordable. Private Wilbur Fisk estimated that the river was about "two feet deep." Alfred Seelye Roe, a veteran of the Ninth New York Heavy Artillery, thought the Potomac "about three feet deep." Some of Wright's veterans viewed the chance to get into the water as a respite from the excessive heat and an opportunity for "fun." Corporal John Rhoades, 110th Ohio Volunteer Infantry, wrote to his wife that she "would have laughed could you have seen the whole division [Brig. Gen. James Ricketts] with pants off, haversacks, bullet pouches slung over their backs, the water only crotch deep in the deepest part." Another veteran in Ricketts's division recorded similarly: "many men cross en dishabille, carrying their clothing on heads or shoulders. Nothing but laughter greets the unfortunate soldiers who step on slimy rocks and receive involuntary immersion." Alanson Haines, chaplain of the 15th New Jersey, thought "the sight of the river, alive with shouting men, was a novel one."

While some reveled in the moment, others wondered if the pursuit would achieve anything. Early's head start, coupled with the belief that the Confederate force was numerically superior, concerned Vermonter Aldace Walker. Despite the belief that the VI Corps contained some of the "best" regiments "in the Army of the Potomac," Walker thought that if Wright's and Early's forces clashed that Wright's troops "would not stand much show against their [Early's] big army." However, Walker believed

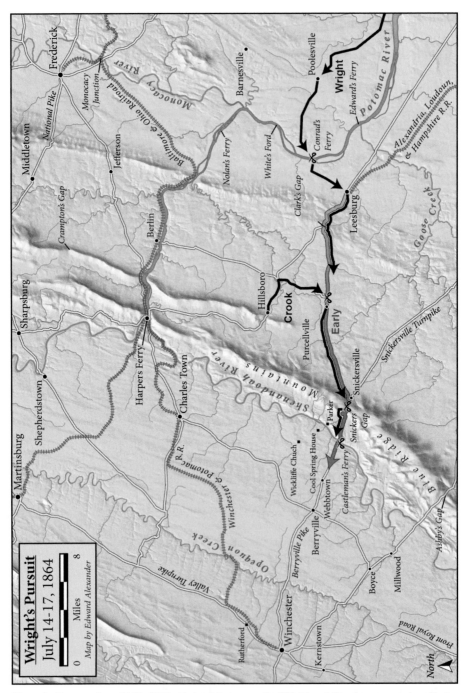

WRIGHT'S PURSUIT, JULY 14-17, 1864—Federal forces under Wright and Crook converged on Early from two directions, triggering several cavalry actions as Early's rear guard tried to buy time for Confederates to pull away.

that a battle between the two armies was unlikely, as the Vermonter did not believe the pursuit force marched at a rapid enough pace to intercept Early. The day after Wright's command crossed the Potomac River, Walker wrote to his father: "we shan't catch 'em I reckon."

As Wright's force crossed the Potomac and marched toward Leesburg on July 16, Crook reached the Department of West Virginia's First Division, as Crook remembered, "about midday" in Hillsboro, a community located approximately ten miles northwest of Leesburg. Crook's arrival seemed to bring a sense of relief to some in the division as it meant Brig. Gen. Jeremiah Sullivan's departure as division commander. A graduate of the United States Naval Academy and attorney in Indiana prior the conflict, some in the Department of West Virginia, including General David Hunter, believed Sullivan lacked ability as a field commander. Jubilant about Sullivan's departure, Col. Joseph Thoburn wrote in his diary on July 16: "I am pleased with Genl. Crook and like the change." Colonel James Mulligan echoed that sentiment. Two days before Crook arrived Mulligan wrote in his diary simply: "don't think much of Sullivan." When Mulligan learned of Crook's appointment on the 16th he wrote jubilantly: "General Sullivan relieved by General Crook. From what I have heard of Crook, change is desirable."

When Crook arrived he inquired as to Early's whereabouts. Unfortunately, Crook learned that "no one knew anything about the enemy." None of this surprised Crook. He believed it a manifestation of Sullivan's incompetence. "It was sufficient to account for all this by the fact that Sullivan was in command . . . in addition to his many other shortcomings," including, as Crook explained, a lack of "actual physical courage." Crook acted quickly to gather as much information as possible about Early's whereabouts. As Crook sent "scouting parties . . . in different directions," Brig. Gen. Alfred Duffié, who commanded the Department of West Virginia's First Cavalry Division and had taken initiative to reconnoiter throughout the morning, reported to Crook that the 5th New York Cavalry, commanded by Lt. Col. Augustus Root, discovered Early's command "moving

Brigadier General Jeremiah Sullivan, a native of Indiana, served in the United States Navy before the Civil War. Those who served under Sullivan in the Shenandoah Valley detested him and thought him incompetent. (loc)

Brigadier General Aflred Duffié was born in Paris, France, in 1835. Before coming to the United States in 1859, he served as a cavalry officer in the French military in Algiers, Senegal, and Crimea. When the Civil War broke out, he received a commission as captain in the 2nd New York Cavalry. He rose to the rank of brigadier general by the summer of 1863. After the Civil War, Duffié served as United States consul in Cadiz, Spain. He held that post until he died in 1880. (loc)

on the Leesburg pike toward Snicker's Gap." Crook immediately ordered Duffié to "send a brigade of cavalry to attack." Duffié chose Col. William Tibbits's brigade. Near Purcellville, approximately eight miles east of Snickers Gap, Tibbits's troopers struck a portion of Early's wagons in the afternoon. Although Tibbits initially seized "200 wagons and about 150 prisoners," the Confederates countered. Troops from Ramseur's and Rodes's divisions reclaimed, according to Duffié's accounting, approximately 100 Confederate soldiers captured by Tibbits and 120 wagons. Of the wagons Tibbits's brigade prevented from being recaptured the troopers burned forty-three, largely "filled with the various kinds of plunder" that Confederates "had . . . stolen in Maryland."

While Duffié praised Tibbits and believed his brigade "entitled to much credit," the attack, in hindsight, amounted to an opportunity lost. The wagons Tibbits attacked were positioned in the center of Early's column. Gordon's and Brig. Gen. Gabriel Wharton's divisions marched in front of the wagon train, while Rodes's and Ramseur's divisions proceeded behind. Had Wright and Crook been aware of the situation and sent reinforcements, Early's army might have been split in two and significantly damaged. Tibbits's attack became, as historian Benjamin Franklin Cooling characterized it, "embarrassing" for the Union pursuers.

The attack seemed to cause little alarm among some in Early's ranks as it continued west toward Snickers Gap and the Shenandoah Valley. Some such as Capt. Cary Whitaker, 43rd North Carolina, believed Tibbits's assault a blessing in disguise as it unburdened the army of various items plundered during Early's march through Maryland which proved of little use to soldiers, including "hoop skirts, calicoes, and such things." Whitaker, while he believed someone was "to blame for this misfortune," admitted to his diary that he "don't care if all such were burned even it if had to be done by the Yankees."

As the threat of attack dissipated that evening, the lead elements of Early's army passed through Snickers Gap and crossed the Shenandoah River. The march from the capital's outskirts back to the Valley, coupled with the aggregate toll of the month's campaigning, left Early's troops exhausted. As the Confederate column stretched from the Shenandoah River's western shore east to Snickers Gap on the night of July 16 Early's command wanted, as Alabamian Henry Beck explained, "much needed rest." However, despite the reality that Early's regiments appeared to possess the upper hand so far, troops in the Army of the Valley harbored no delusions that the Union pursuit would terminate once Confederate troops crossed the Shenandoah River. Early's troops, as an unidentified North Carolinian wrote, "had every reason . . . to anticipate some warm work" in the coming days. That observation proved correct.

"I Hope We Can Whip the Rebs This Summer"

CHAPTER THREE
JULY 17, 1864

The mood among the ranks of the 12th Alabama Infantry seemed somewhat relaxed on the morning of July 17. While much of Early's command passed through Snickers Gap the previous day, the Alabamians picketed the summit of the Blue Ridge Mountains throughout the night. When the regiment received orders to gather gear, shoulder muskets, get into formation, and proceed down the mountain's slopes to the Shenandoah, the Alabamians, according to a soldier in the regiment, "indulged" in "some practical jokes" which "all seemed to enjoy." As the troops crossed the Shenandoah, 1st Lt. Robert Park noted that distractions from war's realities heightened the regiment's mood. "We had a good deal of fun," Park recalled simply.

Confederates already on the Shenandoah's western side hoped the day would afford an opportunity for rest. As Pvt. Henry Hanger, 14th Virginia Cavalry, sat "in a woody grove" in Clarke County, Virginia, he took out a piece of paper and

Modern-day view toward Snickers Gap (jn)

Major General John C. Breckinridge (left) served as vice president of the United States during President James Buchanan's administration. In February 1865 President Jefferson Davis appointed Breckinridge Secretary of War. After the Civil War's end, Breckinridge practiced law in Lexington, Kentucky. He died in 1875. (loc)

Colonel James Mulligan (right) led the only brigade of infantry Duffié had at his disposal on July 17. One week later Mulligan was mortally wounded at the Second Battle of Kernstown. (loc)

wrote a letter to his wife. As he took in the "splendid country" of his native Shenandoah Valley, Hanger explained that Early's army, although "in fine spirits" were "nearly worn out—and must necessarily have a little rest." Throughout the morning and into the early afternoon it appeared that for the first time in over one month Early's command would have an opportunity to relax. Some, such as Maj. Gen. John C. Breckinridge, chose to attend services at Grace Episcopal Church in Berryville, while others worshipped in regimental camps. Having "the pleasure of hearing, for the first time in months, the grand old liturgy of the [Episcopal] Church," energized an unidentified officer from North Carolina. Others took advantage of the hospitality of Confederate civilians who shared meals and camaraderie. One Tar Heel branded it a "pleasant bivouac." However, it did not last long. By early afternoon it became, as a Louisiana chaplain recalled, "another 'Military Sunday.'"

That morning, General Wright ordered Crook "to send a cavalry force to Snickersville, supported by infantry, to push the rear of the enemy column, and ascertain if possible what route they had taken." Crook chose Duffié's cavalry division, Col. James Mulligan's brigade, and a section of Capt. John Keeper's Battery B, 1st West Virginia Light Artillery. Mulligan's two infantry regiments—the 23rd Illinois and 10th West Virginia—led the way. The westward march from Purcellville proved taxing. Colonel Mulligan recorded in his diary simply that the movement to "the foot of the Blue Ridge" was "hard."

Brigadier General George Crook (left) graduated from West Point in 1852. He ranked near the bottom of his graduating class, thirty-eighth out of forty-three. Crook never forgave Maj. Gen. Horatio Wright for not properly supporting troops from his command at Cool Spring. (loc)

Colonel William Tibbits (right), a native of New York, recruited a company of the 2nd New York Infantry after the Confederate attack on Fort Sumter in the spring of 1861. He was commissioned colonel of the 21st New York Cavalry in February 1864. By the time he mustered out of service in 1866, he held the rank of brevet major general. (loc)

As Mulligan's command made the ascent to Snickers Gap he anticipated some resistance. However, aside from a feeble effort by the 37th Virginia Battalion to block the Union advance, Mulligan secured Snickers Gap easily. After Mulligan reached the summit and took in "the valley of mingled gold and green before him," he took out his diary. In addition to reflecting, as he oftentimes did, on how much "joy" his wife Marian and three children brought him, Mulligan pondered why Early's command did not put up "more resistance." Mulligan estimated that the Virginians his brigade encountered fired no more "than half a dozen shots."

With Snickers Gap secured, Mulligan's brigade broke ranks, built fires, made coffee, and watched as Duffié's cavalry and Keeper's cannon passed through the gap and moved down the mountain's western face. Duffié and Tibbitts moved out in advance and reconnoitered the enemy's position. The two found the area around Castleman's Ferry "strongly guarded by infantry and artillery," with Early's "sharpshooters— posted along the banks and hills adjacent."

Additionally, as Col. William Tibbits's and Lt. Col. Gabriel Middleton's brigades descended down the mountain's western face, Tibbits on the right and Middleton on the left, Duffié learned that the nature of the landscape offered the Confederates an additional advantage. Thick woods and brush covered the river's western bank, concealing Gordon's troops, while the mountain slope down which Duffié's force moved was not densely covered and therefore afforded Confederates a clear view. A veteran of the 22nd Pennsylvania Cavalry lamented that the "thinly wooded" mountain "gave the enemy on the opposite side of the river a fine view of our movements."

Gordon's infantry and artillery from Maj. William McLaughlin's artillery battalion, according to one of Duffié's cavalrymen, "opened on us a fierce artillery and musketry fire" as they searched for a suitable position. Lieutenant Colonel Andrew Jackson Greenfield, 22nd Pennsylvania Cavalry, recalled simply that the Confederate artillery fire was "brisk." In addition to confronting bullets and shells, Duffié's command had to contend with parts of trees that transformed into missiles as Confederate artillery shredded the trees on the mountain's western face. "The solid shot," one Union trooper recalled, cut "off the tops and heavy limbs of large pine trees." Some shots struck dead trees which knocked them over completely. One Union soldier recorded that these trees "would fall with a large crash" and placed the men in "constant danger." "Several" of Duffié's men, in the estimation of one Pennsylvania trooper, "were struck by branches of trees cut and falling on them."

As fire from across the river intensified, Duffié's two cavalry brigades hastened into position. Colonel Tibbits, whose brigade proceeded down the mountain's slopes dismounted, took position, as Tibbitts recalled, "near the ford [Castleman's Ferry] . . . on the high ground above it—in the timber" on the south side of the Berryville Pike. The section from Keeper's battery situated itself on the pike's north side, as Tibbitts remembered, "on still higher ground." Once in position Keeper's guns opened fire. Around 2:00 p.m., according to Father James Sheeran, the chaplain of the 14th Louisiana, "the Yankees made their appearance on the heights on the opposite side of the Shenandoah" and began "to shell our camp." The fire from Keeper's three-inch ordnance rifles unnerved Sheeran. As the chaplain hid "behind a large oak tree" he noticed that the initial rounds from Keeper's guns seemed to have little effect on General Gordon's troops. "They coolly and leisurely finished their frugal meal and then fell into line of battle," Sheeran wrote.

Two cannons from McLaughlin's battalion situated on a piece of high ground near North Hill

Plantation south of the Berryville Pike responded to Keeper's guns. The artillery fire became so intense that it could be heard miles away. From the camp of the 14th Virginia Cavalry, located between Millwood and Winchester, approximately a dozen miles to the west, Pvt. Henry Hanger wrote to his wife, "I hear some little cannonading supposed to be beyond [Snickers] Gap."

Castleman's Ferry as it appeared around 1900. (jn)

Fire from Gordon's "sharpshooters" also intensified. As 1st Lt. Joseph Isenberg, the adjutant of the 22nd Pennsylvania Cavalry, positioned troops, he thought the Confederates concentrated an unusually fierce musketry fire in the area around him. This puzzled Isenberg momentarily. Isenberg quickly realized that the regiment's commanding officer, Lt. Col. Andrew Jackson Greenfield, stuck out conspicuously in his "light coat" and attracted extra attention. As "the bullets were striking the trees and bank beyond us," Greenfield recalled that Isenberg shouted: "They are shooting at that light jacket; I'm going to get away from you."

While Isenberg sought a safer place that afternoon, Duffié contemplated his next move. Initially, Duffié sent a messenger to Mulligan, who was "dining" at the time and "listen[ing] to the roar" of battle from his bivouac in Snickers Gap, and requested support from "some" of Mulligan's infantry. Mulligan sent

Colonel Thomas Harris, 10th West Virginia Infantry, was promoted to brevet brigadier general on October 19, 1864. (loc)

Col. Thomas M. Harris's 10th West Virginia Infantry. No sooner had Mulligan given Harris the order to move to the cavalry's aid, another of Duffié's couriers arrived requesting Mulligan to "bring all your infantry forward immediately." As Mulligan's small brigade maneuvered into position, Confederate artillery lobbed shells into the Union infantry. Among those victimized was Pvt. Isaac Burkhammer, Company C, 10th West Virginia Infantry. In the battle's aftermath Pvt. Levi Lockard, who served in the same company, wrote to Burkhammer's family and shared the wretched news that Burkhammer was "killed by a cannon shot."

Burkhammer, a twenty-six-year-old farmer from Lewis County, West Virginia, enlisted in the regiment in March 1862. The news saddened not only Burkhammer's mother and father, Elizabeth and Leonard, but also his new bride Marth Angeline. The couple had married on January 21, 1864. One month after Burkhammer's death the seventeen-year-old widow filed a claim for a widow's pension. The United States government approved Martha's claim on November 22, 1864. Martha received $8 per month, the standard rate awarded to widows of privates, until she remarried on April 25, 1867. Interestingly, once Martha was no longer permitted to receive a widow's pension, Burkhammer's mother attemped to claim a dependent's pension. On June 7, 1890, Elizabeth claimed that her son "left neither widow nor child." While true he left no children, her claim that he left no widow was erroneous. She contended that as the eldest of three children, Isaac provided considerable financial support for the family, particularly after her husband Leonard fell off a horse and suffered a debilitating injury. The government rejected Elizabeth's claim in early January 1895. Thirteen years later, Private Burkhammer's sister submitted a claim as a dependent. Confronting economic hardship and illness, Matilda Burkhammer believed her brother's sacrifice at Snickers Gap might offer some financial relief to someone so "old and feeble and sickly." The government denied Matilda's claim.

As Union troops stood on the Shenandoah's eastern side that afternoon and confronted fire from Confederate artillery and Gordon's troops, both Colonels Mulligan and Tibbits suggested a more advantageous position for Keeper's artillery. Initially, Duffié accepted Tibbits's advice and moved Keeper's section to "an elevated position" on the south side of the Berryville Pike that Tibbits believed "commanded the enemy's artillery." Although Duffié thought it initially a sound idea, one that might help break the Confederate stronghold, his perspective shifted by the time the section from Battery B, 1st West Virginia Light Artillery reached its new position. Considering the strength of his command and that of the enemy's, Duffié thought it unwise to attack. Colonel Tibbits recalled that the West Virginians "had hardly opened when" Duffié realized "that it was foolhardy to attempt a crossing." Although Duffié possessed a reputation as aggressive, something put on full display the previous day as he struck Early's wagon train, Duffié thought it unlikely his command, without additional support, could successfully dislodge Castleman's Ferry's defenders. Eleven days later Duffié explained that with "the enemy posted in considerable force . . . their artillery and infantry completely commanding the ford," he determined to disengage and move back to Snickers Gap. In addition to the strength of the Confederate defense, Duffié also considered the tired and famished condition of his command's horses. He later explained in defense of his decision that he needed "to find water and grass for my horses" and that the day's events left his division's steeds "very much jaded."

Some did not believe the decision to disengage prudent, among them Colonel Mulligan. As he "devoured with greed" a "leg and breast of chicken" late that night in the safety of Snickers Gap, Mulligan believed his brigade "humiliated" by Duffié's decision to withdraw. Mulligan confided to his diary, "I've had enough of Duffié's management." Mulligan's perspective did not change overnight. That morning he again groused in his diary: "I've had enough of Duffié and any other General without . . . judgment."

Once Duffié determined to withdraw, he next needed to decide at what time to begin the trek east, back up the mountain's slopes. Making the move in daylight proved equally risky and so he waited until dark to begin the movement. While a Confederate chaplain recorded that the "firing ceased about 6 p.m." accounts from Union veterans state that much of Duffié's command remained

Andrew Jackson Greenfield (left) received his commission as lieutenant colonel of the 22nd Pennsylvania Cavalry on March 24, 1864. After the Civil War, he was elected mayor of Oil City, Pennsylvania. He also received an appointment as postmaster of Oil City by President Grover Cleveland. Greenfield died in 1931. (scf)

Major George T. Work (right), a native of Washington County, Pennsylvania, was born in 1825. As a child, Work devoured histories of the American Revolution and War of 1812. In the years before the conflict, Work joined the Winfield Hussars, a local cavalry company. When the Civil War broke out, the Hussars became Company I, 1st Pennsylvania Cavalry. After overcoming a severe bout of pneumonia in the spring of 1862, Work received permission from Governor Andrew Curtin to recruit what eventually became Company C, 22nd Pennsylvania Cavalry. Work was commissioned major of the regiment on March 25, 1864. (scf)

in position and exchanged fire with Confederates until dark. For example, Lt. Col. Andrew Jackson Greenfield, 22nd Pennsylvania Cavalry, remembered that Keeper's "artillery and Colonel Mulligan's Infantry and" a contingent of "dismounted cavalry . . . kept up a desultory fire until dark," and then Duffié's command withdrew.

Duffié's entire command, however, did not move east toward Snickers Gap. A contingent of the 22nd Pennsylvania Cavalry established, as trooper Samuel Farrar recalled, "a strong picket . . . near the ford." Around midnight Maj. John T. Work gathered a portion of the Pennsylvanians, hoping to catch the Confederates sleeping, and attempted to cross. As soon as Work's men stepped into the Shenandoah River a "volley was poured into them," according to one cavalryman. Perhaps somewhat remarkably, "the terrific musketry fire" only struck one soldier in Work's detachment—Pvt. John Sanders. A member of the regiment for approximately three-and-a-half months, Sanders died from his wounds eight days later. He became the seventeenth, and final, casualty of the initial effort to capture Castleman's Ferry. Following the failed effort, Work reported to Duffié what the cavalry division commander already knew—"that they [Confederates] were in strong force."

That night troops on both sides took stock of the day's "sharp engagement." Union soldiers who had little combat experience, such as the 22nd Pennsylvania Cavalry's Samuel Farrar, believed that the fighting on July 17 was not " a skirmish" but "a severe engagement." Comrade Sergeant John Elwood, a veteran of the 22nd Pennsylvania, who had served in the Union cavalry since June 29, 1861, branded the fight "a brisk brush." Chauncey Norton, a battle-tested veteran of the 15th New York Cavalry, thought the fighting that day nothing more than "a little skirmish." Although not engaged in the battle, Confederate artillerist Milton Humphreys, whose camp rested "not more than 1 ½ miles from" Castleman's Ferry, believed the incessant exchange of small arms and artillery fire signaled "considerable fighting."

Regardless of how soldiers might have characterized the fighting on July 17, the action that day concerned General Early. At 10:00 p.m. Early sent a message to Breckinridge directing him to have Brig. Gen. John Echols's brigade, Gordon's division, and artillery "under arms at daylight." Early wanted Gordon's division to protect Castleman's Ferry with Echols in support. "Have his [Gordon's] troops on the watch," Early instructed, "and if any attempt at crossing is made" Early wanted Gordon's regiments to make "the most determined resistance."

Meanwhile in Clark's Gap, thirteen miles east of Snickers Gap, Wright seemed convinced "that the enemy is in full retreat for Richmond." Wright, however, needed to be certain before he ended his pursuit of Early. That evening Wright formulated a plan for the following day. He directed Crook to "move at 4 a.m. on the Snickersville pike to Snickersville, and through Snicker's Gap." Additionally, Wright instructed "Brigadier General-James Ricketts, with the VI Corps," to "move at the same hour over the same route." Finally, Wright ordered, "Brigadier-General William Emory, with his command [a portion of the XIX Corps], will move at the same hour to Clark's Gap and follow the other commands."

As orders trickled into Crook's command, encamped in Purcellville seven miles east of Snickers Gap, some pondered how effectively they would fight if they encountered the enemy. All that these regiments had been through since suffering defeat at Lynchburg in June left Crook's troops exhausted. A veteran of the 123rd Ohio Infantry described the regiment as "sleepy" on July 17 as a result of the "severe marching and physical endurance of the

Colonel Joseph Thoburn, a physician by training, was arguably one of the best division commanders who ever commanded troops in the Shenandoah Valley. After Thoburn perished from a mortal wound he received at the battle of Cedar Creek on October 19, 1864, the Central Union Club of Wheeling, West Virginia, issued a resolution that praised Thoburn as a "gallant . . . true patriot and model soldier, a man of noble and honorable impulse." (np)

past two months." Duties performed on July 17 under a "red hot" sun exacerbated their condition. After "Sunday morning inspection" Cpl. Charles Lynch, 18th Connecticut Infantry, recorded in his diary that contingents of Union soldiers carried out orders to burn "large stacks of grain in this vicinity to prevent the enemy from getting [it]. It made a hot fire and a great loss." While Lynch understood the value of preventing its use by Confederate troops, he lamented that the destruction would burden area civilians. "It will no doubt cause much suffering among the people. Women and children in these parts suffer by the war which is a cruel thing," Lynch recorded in his diary on the 17th.

Exhaustion aside, the condition of some of the regiments in Crook's command was deplorable. Colonel Joseph Thoburn confided to his diary that day: "We are out of provisions and in poor condition." A Connecticut soldier echoed: "We are getting very ragged. Many are barefooted. Clothes will wear out in this rough life." Efforts had been made earlier in the day to resupply Crook's troops, but the effort failed to fully refit the troops with all they needed. William Walker, the chaplain of the 18th Connecticut, noted that "rations and some clothing and shoes were issued" on the morning of July 17 "but not enough of the latter to meet the demand." Walker observed that "there were a large number of men barefoot, or in a worse condition, with shoes so extremely poor and hard they galled the feet of their owners." William McMurphy, a veteran of the 7th Michigan Cavalry who served as part of a provisional brigade of dismounted cavalry commanded by Col. Samuel Young, also complained about the worn out condition of his shoes. McMurphy, who earlier in the conflict served in the 1st Michigan Infantry and was injured at the battle of Malvern Hill when a tree fell on him, bemoaned to his mother in a letter penned from Purcellville on the night of July 17: "I. . . . don't know how long I can march if we make long marches. . . . My feet are one mass of blisters." As much as McMurphy admitted that this pursuit of Early had made him "sick of soldiering" he looked forward to impending battle and the opportunity to be part of an army that defeated Early. "The hopes of using up the Johnnys this summer is good as a plaster for my feet."

Despite orders that Crook's regiments would have to rise before daybreak and be on the march west toward Snickers Gap by 4:00 a.m., some took the opportunity that night to gather in their camps and sing. In the 18th Connecticut's camp, Chaplain Walker recalled, "the boys had one of their old-fashioned social singing meetings." For approximately one hour the air "rang with the sound of vocal music" and then the gathering broke up and the men went to sleep. Sadly, however, as Chaplain Walker later reflected, some did not realize that that night would be their last moment of revelry and "their last sleep."

"Send a Force Across the River"

CHAPTER FOUR
JULY 18, 1864
3:00 A.M. – 4:00 P.M.

As the sound of reveille pierced the early morning air at 3:00 a.m. on July 18 in the Union camps in Purcellville, Virginia, Cpl. Charles Lynch, 18th Connecticut, seemed ready for the early-morning march to Snickers Gap. "Up & early on the march this fine morning . . . pushing on . . . in the direction of Snicker's Gap," Lynch penned in his diary. Not all shared his enthusiasm. Half of Lynch's regimental comrades could not make the march. Some were physically exhausted, others ill, and some without shoes. Of the approximately 200 men in the 18th Connecticut who reported for roll call that morning, "about one hundred, sick and barefoot" soldiers, according to the regimental chaplain, were deemed unfit for duty and sent to Harpers Ferry. The problems which the 18th Connecticut confronted permeated throughout Crook's command.

Although he refused to leave his regiment, Lt. Col. Elijah E. Massey, 2nd Maryland Eastern Shore Infantry, complained to Col. Thoburn about the

Living historians deploy as skirmishers at Island Ford during the 155th anniversary commemoration of Cool Spring. (jn)

Corporal Charles Lynch enlisted in the 18th Connecticut on August 6, 1862. A veteran of twenty-five battles and skirmishes, Lynch calculated that during the fighting in the Shenandoah Valley in 1864 he marched "every step" of the 1,300 miles his regiment covered. (cl)

debilitating impact of the previous month's marching and fighting. The sixty-year-old Massey, who suffered from "a disease of the kidneys & bladder," explained to Thoburn: "From the severe exposure during our long march to Lynchburg and back my physical strength has become entirely exhausted." Keenly aware of the horrid condition of his troops, Thoburn lamented in his diary: "We are out of provisions and in poor condition to pursue."

At 4:00 a.m. Crook "agreeably to orders . . . proceeded" west. As Crook's regiments made the seven-mile march to Snickers Gap, followed by the remainder of Wright's command, debris from Early's army and clashes over the previous two days littered the road. "All along the way were seen . . . dead horses and fragments of broken wagons," recalled a veteran of the 18th Connecticut. While the scene, particularly that of dead animals, repulsed some Union soldiers, the odor of rotting animal carcasses proved particularly revolting. "The stench from the swollen carcasses lying under the sweltering rays of the hot July sun was terrific," recalled Pvt. George Perkins, 149th Ohio Infantry. Perkins explained that the soldiers "hurried past" one particular field where the odor was nauseating "as fast as possible, breathing a sigh of relief when we came again into the pure air." Disgusting scenes and the revolting pong sobered some Union soldiers to the reality that battle appeared imminent. One of Crook's veterans wrote simply: "Things began to look more serious, and every hours march lessened the distance between conflicting forces."

As Union troops marched west some broke ranks and foraged for food along the route. One Ohio soldier recalled that he "saw a squad of soldiers" attempting to capture a cow. As two soldiers tied a rope around its horns and others got behind and tried to push it, an unidentified woman to whom the cow belonged, and her children, begged the Union troops to leave it alone. Other troops pursued less ambitious foraging goals. When Crook's regiments arrived in Snickersville, situated along the eastern base of the Blue Ridge Mountains, around 9:00 a.m. some foraged for honey. Private Benjamin Bogardus, 170th Ohio Infantry, explained that Snickersville "was a great place for honey, the best" he "ever saw."

While some of Crook's troops foraged and others rested near Snickersville, Crook proceeded up the mountain's slopes to Snickers Gap. Colonel James Mulligan was among the first to greet Crook when he arrived. Mulligan, who described Crook in his diary that day as a "very quiet, and very unobtrusive gentleman," rode with Crook to a point on the mountain where they could see the Confederate position at Castleman's Ferry. As Crook made his way to the mountain's summit, Maj. George T. Work and a contingent of seventy-five cavalrymen readied themselves for an attack against Castleman's Ferry. Earlier that morning General Duffié ordered Work to "cross the river," insisting that "only a heavy picket" defended the strategic crossing. Work believed the directive futile. Every effort to seize Castleman's Ferry the previous day terminated in failure. Furthermore, Work believed Duffié underestimated the strength of the Confederate force defending Castleman's Ferry. When Work informed the men of their task that morning, one Pennsylvanian recalled that Work "called the officers and read the order, pointing out what we all knew—the impossibility of executing the order." As much as he disagreed with Duffié and anticipated the failed outcome, Work believed "duty" required him "to obey."

Work believed that if the mission had any chance of success, he needed to divide his command into thirds and attempt to cross the river at three different points. Work directed 2nd Lt. Felix Crago, in command of twenty-five men, to cross the Shenandoah River approximately 100 yards north of Castleman's Ferry. A second contingent of twenty-five men commanded by Capt. James Y. Chessrown was directed to cross about 100 yards south of Castleman's Ferry. The remaining twenty-five troopers, under Work's command, would attempt to cross at Castleman's Ferry. The Pennsylvanians did not come under fire from Confederates guarding Castleman's Ferry, troops in Brig. Gen. Zebulon York's command and artillery from Maj. William McLaughlin's battalion, until they entered the Shenandoah River. One trooper recalled "just as we got into the river the enemy opened on us with their batteries." The cavalrymen responded and

Lieutenant Colonel Elijah Massey, 2nd Maryland Eastern Shore, was sixty-one at the time of the battle. Ailed by kidney and bladder disease, the march from the nation's capital to the Shenandoah Valley proved too much for Massey physically. He was discharged from the service on October 31, 1864. Massey died on January 22, 1871. (dbs)

Born in Maine in 1819, Brig. Gen. Zebulon York commanded a brigade of Louisiana regiments in Early's army. York was wounded at the Third Battle of Winchester. (loc)

exchanged fire with York's regiments. Shortly after the Pennsylvanians opened fire, Confederate infantry defending the important crossing took cover on the ground and behind trees. Private Felix Bledsoe, 9th Louisiana Infantry, wrote ten days after the battle that the "yankees fired from the opposite bank of the river. . . . We all fell upon the ground, and then sought trees upon the bank of the river." As soldiers in the 9th Louisiana took cover, Capt. Reuben Allen Pierson, commanding the regiment's picket line along the Shenandoah's western bank, "walked along perfectly regardless of dangers" and according to Private Bledsoe "exclaimed 'Boys see those Yankees . . . shoot them.'"

The son of one of the largest plantation owners in Bienville, Louisiana, and one of four brothers who fought for the Confederacy, Capt. Pierson had just returned to the regiment two days earlier after recovering from a gunshot wound he received to his right hand at the battle of the Wilderness. That morning Pierson appeared, in the estimation of one of his men, oblivious to the "dangers . . . too boisterous and too much destitute of caution and craftiness." While Pierson might have seemed unfazed by Work's troopers, the reality that he was the only member of the 9th Louisiana exposed and "giving orders . . . in his usual loud tone" attracted the attention of Work's command. Private Bledsoe recalled that "25 Yankees were within 100 & 150 yards of him" and fired in Pierson's direction. One of those bullets struck Pierson's right arm and passed through his body. After he was shot, Pvt. Philip Collins, Pierson's cousin, rushed to his aid. However, there was little Collins could do as the wound proved mortal. "He only spoke twice after he fell. He spoke to me and said [sic] he was killed dead to take him out and he died immediately," Collins explained to Pierson's father William ten days later. Collins buried Pierson in the Shepherd family graveyard near Berryville. After the war, Pierson's remains were reinterred in Winchester's Stonewall Confederate Cemetery.

The stubborn Confederate defense of Castleman's Ferry that morning forced Work's contingent to withdraw. As the Pennsylvanians fell back and reflected on their most recent effort to cross the river, they seemed astonished that despite furious salvos from the enemy's artillery, none of it struck Work's cavalrymen. The reality that not one of the seventy-five men were killed astounded Pvt. Samuel Clarke Farrar. "How we ever got out is a mystery to me," Farrar wrote, "but strange to say none were killed." Farrar surmised that the reason for the Pennsylvanians' good fortune was that the Confederate gunners "aimed too high." Although the Confederate artillery inflicted no direct damage on Work's command, shells that cut tree branches, just as had been the case the previous day, injured "several" troopers. Additionally, Lt. Isaac M. Regester was injured during the retreat when his horse fell on him. Regester suffered "a badly bruised leg" and an injury to his spine. He coped with those ailments for the remainder of his life. On June 6, 1898, the day after Regester died at West Penn Hospital in Pittsburgh, the *Pittsburgh Daily Post* reported that the injury he received to his spine in 1864 "superinduced" the lingering illness that killed him.

Following the failed attack, Work sent Lt. Crago to find Crook and tell him that the effort failed. When Crago reached Crook he found the general "sitting on a log, surrounded by a number of flashily-dressed young officers . . . wearing a common blouse." Unbeknownst to Crago, Crook watched the entire attack. After Crago delivered his report Crook informed him that although the Pennsylvanians could not secure Castleman's Ferry, Crook believed that Work's troopers "had done all that men could have done under the circumstances."

After two days of failed attempts to cross the Shenandoah River at Castleman's Ferry, Crook thought that the Union cavalry could be put to better use by sending them nine miles south to Ashby's Gap. Crook hoped that Duffié's regiments could "pass through Ashby's Gap and attack the enemy train in flank." The cavalrymen departed around 1:00 p.m. and reached Ashby's Gap the following day. Unfortunately for Duffié's command, Confederates stubbornly defended Ashby's Gap and prevented Duffié from carrying out his objective successfully.

As Duffié's column rode south, Wright and Crook conferred atop the Blue Ridge about what to do next. The problem that both generals confronted was that they "could not tell," according to Crook, whether Early's troops "were in force or not." Despite Crook's belief "that only the enemy's cavalry were holding" the strategic crossing, he did not believe another direct assault the most prudent decision. Wright and Crook agreed to flank the Confederate position by crossing the Shenandoah River at Island Ford, approximately two miles north of Castleman's Ferry, turning south, and driving Early's defenders from Castleman's Ferry.

Crook turned to Col. Joseph Thoburn to carry out the flank attack. With three infantry brigades and a provisional brigade of dismounted cavalry, Thoburn's troops climbed the mountain to Snickers Gap. When Thoburn's brigades reached the summit around 1:00 p.m. the beauty of the Shenandoah Valley's landscape in front of them and the equally breathtaking Loudoun Valley to their rear left them in awe. "The scene was both inspiring and exciting. From that point could be seen the beautiful valleys of Loudon on the one hand, and the Shenandoah on the other," wrote a veteran of the 18th Connecticut. Another soldier who glimpsed the Shenandoah Valley for the first time that day recalled: "That day [July 18, 1864] we obtained our first view of the celebrated Valley of the Shenandoah. . . . The surrounding country dotted with house and groves and waving fields. . . . the occasional glimpses of the blue Shenandoah rushing past the very foot of the mountain. . . . and the blue hills bounding the landscape where it faded into indistinctness, made up a most glorious view, scarcely equaled on the continent in its mellow beauty."

Thoburn received his final instructions around 2:00 p.m. to take his command of approximately 5,000 men, cross the Shenandoah River at Island Ford, turn south, and "dislodge a force of the enemy" Thoburn's superiors "supposed to be cavalry." The difficulty Thoburn confronted was how to effectively navigate the unfamiliar rugged mountainous terrain and reach Island Ford. Fortuitously, the Union force which had been pursuing Early's army contained a soldier who knew this area in Clarke County, Virginia, quite well: John Carrigan.

Born in New York City circa 1818 (Carrigan's birth year varies), Carrigan resided in Clarke County near Castleman's Ferry where he worked as a tailor in the decades prior to the Civil War. Known to his friends as "Barney," Carrigan possessed a reputation as an excellent musician. An unidentified friend who reminisced about Carrigan on June 20, 1888, four days after Carrigan committed suicide by "cutting his throat with a razor while suffering from temporary aberration of the mind" at his home near Boyce in Clarke County, lauded Carrigan for the "soul stirring music" he played on his "fife and Maddox's drum." On April 18, 1861, the day after Virginia's secession convention voted in favor of severing the Old Dominion's bond with the United States, Carrigan enlisted as a musician in Company I, 2nd Virginia Infantry. For reasons unclear Carrigan deserted from the regiment on March 11, 1862, the date Confederate General Thomas J. "Stonewall" Jackson, evacuated Winchester. While nothing indicates Carrigan's whereabouts for the next twenty-one months, he enlisted in the 3rd Maryland Potomac Home Brigade on January 3, 1864, in Monrovia, Maryland. Carrigan served as the regiment's chief musician until he mustered out on May 29, 1865.

What compelled Carrigan to enlist in a Confederate regiment, desert, and then nearly two years later join a Union regiment is unclear. Perhaps Carrigan fell into that category of white southern Unionists who eventually joined Union regiments, but earlier in the conflict enlisted in Confederate units to create the illusion of Confederate loyalty in an area so staunchly Confederate for reasons of self-preservation. Another possibility is that Carrigan, someone an unidentified friend hoped would "be remembered as a true and faithful Confederate soldier," grew disenchanted with the Confederate war effort and switched allegiances. Although not common, it is not, as historian Richard Nelson Current concluded in his classic study Lincoln's Loyalists, entirely unique. Regardless of Carrigan's motivation he became one of nearly 38,000 Virginians to don Union blue during the conflict.

Although the 3rd Maryland Potomac Home Brigade was not part of Thoburn's command, it served as part of General Wright's pursuit force— one of three infantry regiments in an independent brigade commanded by Brig. Gen. John Kenly and attached to Brig. Gen. William Emory's XIX Corps. Whether Crook or Thoburn were aware of Carrigan's connections to the area or Carrigan offered his services to guide Thoburn's troops is unknown.

Carrigan guided Thoburn's four brigades north along what one of Thoburn's veterans characterized as "a narrow cart path" in the mountain "under cover of hills and woods, unobserved by the enemy" to its junction with Parker's Ford Road which passed in front of the Retreat—a stately home constructed in 1799 and at the time of the battle owned by Judge Richard Parker, the judge who presided over John Brown's trial in the autumn of 1859. As Thoburn's command, led by Col. George Wells's brigade, marched down Parker's Ford Road, traversed the ground of Parker's Retreat, and approached the Shenandoah River's shoreline, the sound of artillery boomed in the distance.

To the south, on an eminence approximately "two hundred feet above the river," cannon from Battery L, 5th United States Artillery commanded by 1st Lt. Gulian V. Weir directed fire, according to a newspaper correspondent for the *New York Herald* assigned to Wright's command, at "a few" Confederate wagons "at several different places west of Castleman's Ferry." As the "splendid shots" crashed near the wagons Thoburn's command approached Island Ford.

Modern-day view of "The Retreat." Thoburn's troops marched down the road situated to the left of the home en route to Island Ford. (jn)

Colonel Wells's lead regiment, the 34th Massachusetts, expected no resistance at the crossing; however, when they approached within 200 yards of the Shenandoah River's eastern shore, approximately 100 troops from the 42nd Virginia and 50th Virginia commanded by Maj. Jesse Richardson opened fire. Concealed in bushes which lined the river's bank, Richardson's men, according to a soldier in the 12th West Virginia, "opened a brisk fire." When the report of musketry fire at Island Ford reached Weir's ears he ordered his battery to continue firing so as to distract the enemy's attention from Thoburn's mission. "Skirmishing was now heard at Island ford, and Weir kept his guns in play to assist in the crossing," recalled a newspaper correspondent positioned near Weir's battery.

It would, however, take more than Weir's diversion to allow Thoburn's regiments to cross successfully. As Thoburn quickly surveyed the situation he was troubled that "the banks of the river for some distance above and below the fording were well veiled by trees and bushes, behind which the enemy were posted." Instead of crossing at Island Ford against a well-concealed and, as a veteran of the 12th West Virginia wrote three days later, "advantageously posted" Confederate force of undeterminable strength, Thoburn sought an alternative crossing. As

Modern-day view of Island Ford where troops from Col. George Wells's brigade clashed with Maj. Jesse Richardson's command. (jn)

Colonel George Wells and his brigade led Thoburn's advance to the Shenandoah River. Wells was mortally wounded on October 13, 1864, during a small clash south of Middletown, Virginia. (jn)

two infantry companies remained in front of Island Ford to "engage the attention of the enemy," troops from the 34th Massachusetts Infantry and 5th New York Heavy Artillery moved to "a good fording some distance below" Island Ford and "pushed across."

Once Wells's command reached the Shenandoah River's western shore it drove Richardson's troops from the river's bank. Wells's regiments pushed Richardson's Virginians, in the estimation of a veteran of the 34th Massachusetts, "some half mile to the cover of some woods." While most of Richardson's command escaped, Wells's troops captured some Virginians, including a captain who served on the staff of General Early's chief of artillery, Brig. Gen. Armistead L. Long. Although Wells's troops captured Confederate troops that afternoon, the actual number of Confederates taken prisoner varies slightly. Colonel Thoburn reported a dozen captured in his diary on July 19. Ten days later Thoburn wrote in his official report that Wells captured sixteen men. A veteran of the 34th Massachusetts recorded they captured twenty-one. Wells's command suffered one man killed and another wounded during the crossing.

Regardless of the precise number of Confederates captured, Thoburn gathered what he believed to be vital information from them. "From the prisoners," Thoburn recalled, "I learned that there had been two regiments of rebel infantry guarding the ford, and also that the divisions of the rebel Generals Gordon and Rodes were within a mile or two of the ford, and that General Early was present." With such a large presence of Confederates nearby and the Shenandoah River, once Thoburn crossed his brigades to the river's western shore, separating his command from the rest of the Union force, Thoburn thought it prudent to send an aide to General Crook and inform him of the situation before he turned his regiments south to attack Castleman's Ferry. When Crook learned from Thoburn that much more than a contingent of "the enemy's cavalry" guarded the crossing, Crook conferred with General Wright. In agreement that Thoburn should no longer move south to Castleman's Ferry, Wright ordered the VI Corps "to support" Thoburn's brigades. While the VI Corps made its way down the mountain's slopes Crook instructed

Thoburn to "take as strong a position as possible near" Island Ford "and await the arrival of a division of the Sixth Corps."

As Thoburn questioned the prisoners, relaying what he learned to his superiors, and Wright adjusted Thoburn's objective, Thoburn's brigades crossed to the Shenandoah's western side. Despite the river's low water levels, a soldier in the 123rd Ohio noted that though the "river was waist deep," the crossing was not without its perils. As Pvt. John Gundy, 170th Ohio, waded across the river he "rang against a snag" in the river. In Gundy's attempt to free his left leg from whatever snagged him, he ruptured his groin. Infection soon followed and prompted his discharge from the regiment on September 10, 1864. Gundy never recovered. He died on October 30, 1864.

Another member of the 170th Ohio, William Rankin, who was "partially recovered" from measles contracted while serving in the defenses of Washington, became, in the estimation of his company commander, Capt. Nathan Rowles, chilled "from wading in the river" that afternoon and "was again taken ill." Doctors who tended to Rankin in Baltimore connected his death on August 11, 1864, to the river crossing that afternoon.

Although not quite as tragic, the march to Island Ford and the river crossing pushed Lt. Col. Elijah Massey to his physical limits. The Marylander, who lamented his poor physical condition to Col. Thoburn, contended that the march and "fording the Shenandoah on the 18th" had "so much increased" his exhaustion. The regiment's assistant surgeon, Ezekiel Cooper, agreed. Massey, Cooper explained, "has been greatly increased by the fatigue and exposure of the recent severe march . . . [and] he is in my opinion unfit for duty." Gundy's, Rankin's, and Massey's experiences underscore the reality that all Civil War soldiers confronted an additional enemy: the environment.

With Thoburn's brigades on the Shenandoah's western shore by approximately 4:00 p.m., he arrayed his command. While his skirmishers deployed on an upland ridge just east of the Cool Spring mansion, Thoburn organized his command into two lines. He established one line in "an old road" which ran along the river's bank. A "low stone fence" on the road's western edge "afforded," in Thoburn's estimation, "excellent protection." About seventy-yards from the river's edge "under the cover of a bluff that ran parallel to . . . the river," Thoburn positioned his other line. As this line formed in fields planted with wheat and dotted with stone walls and limestone outcroppings, obstacles which some soldiers used for protection, it followed the sloping land's contours. Instead of being a straight line, it appeared more like an arc. Colonel Daniel Frost's brigade anchored the center. Colonel Wells's brigade guarded the southern flank. Colonel Thoburn's brigade and Col. Samuel Young's provisional brigade of dismounted cavalry protected the northern flank.

As Thoburn's regiments moved into position, some believed, as the 18th Connecticut's Charles Lynch wrote in his diary, that "battle seems to be imminent." Others were not quite so certain and remained hopeful that the contested crossing at Island Ford would be the only engagement that day. A veteran of the 4th West Virginia Infantry explained in a letter the following day that Thoburn's command "lay for nearly an hour without any show of hostility and indeed without scarcely any indication of the enemy in our front."

View looking from the Shenandoah River's eastern bank to its western side. After crossing the Shenandoah River at Island Ford, Thoburn arrayed his command in two main lines, one along the river's edge, and another on a ridge approximately seventy-five yards from the river's shore. (jn)

During that respite of approximately "one hour," some of Thoburn's veterans readied themselves for a fight, while others turned their attention to loved ones at home. Colonel Daniel Frost took the opportunity to visit his brother-in-law, Pvt. James McDonald, who served in the 170th Ohio. Frost proudly showed McDonald, married to Frost's sister Kate, "some new photographs of his family that he had just received." As Frost shared the images with McDonald, Pvt. Benjamin Bogardus claimed to overhear Frost express how much he had grown tired of the conflict and that "he would give his interest in the Government to see them again." Although no record exists as to what particularly made Frost grow weary, perhaps the death of his two-week old daughter Martha on May 1, 1864, contributed to it. Sensing despondency in Frost's voice, Pvt. McDonald assured Frost that things would be alright and he would soon be reunited with his wife Ellen and three children Bushrod, Daniel, and Arthur. Do "not . . . feel bad," McDonald said in comfort. McDonald attempted to assure Frost that "he had got through all right so far, and he would still." As Frost shared his grief with his brother-in-law, Rodes's division, encamped near Wickliffe Church approximately two miles northwest of where Thoburn's command crossed, prepared to march toward Island Ford. Throughout the morning Rodes's troops, as the 43rd North Carolina's 2nd Lt. William Beavans recorded in his diary, "remained very quietly in camp" or spent the time, as the 5th Alabama's Joel Calvin McDiarmid recalled, "foraging" throughout the "nice rich country" where "milk, etc. are plenty." Although no specific threat, save the attempt to cross at Castleman's Ferry, materialized, Rodes's troops received orders around 1:00 p.m. to be ready to move at any instant. Henry Beck, 5th Alabama, recorded in his diary: "At 1 p.m. received orders to be ready to move at a moment's warning." About three hours later, as Thoburn's brigades crossed the Shenandoah, Rodes's division received, as one Alabamian remembered, "orders to move immediately."

As Rodes's command marched toward the Shenandoah River, Brig. Gen. Gabriel Wharton's division, encamped near Webbtown about four miles from Castleman's Ferry, proceeded toward

Little did Col. Daniel Frost realize as he visited with his brother-in-law on the afternoon of July 18 that he would be mortally wounded hours later. (ahec)

At the time Thoburn's division crossed the Shenandoah River, Rodes's division encamped near Wickliffe Church, approximately two miles northwest of Island Ford. (jn)

the Shenandoah River. As Wharton's brigades marched eastward, they came under fire from Weir's battery. Second Lieutenant William Ashley, a native of Chester, England who served in Company C, Thomas' Legion, recorded in his diary that they "marched, under heavy artillery fire, closer to the enemy." Although unnerved by the artillery fire and troubled that Weir's artillery wounded "several" members of his company, he admired the accuracy of Weir's battery. "They are splendid artillerists," Ashley wrote in his diary. A correspondent for the *New York Daily Herald* who observed events that afternoon wrote that as Wharton's brigades "came within range of our guns on the hill . . . Weir's battery made some of the best shots ever seen in artillery practice."

From their perch atop the mountain, Wright and Crook spied Confederate troops moving toward the Shenandoah River. "The dust began to rise in two or three different quarters," one observer recorded, "and from our lookout on the hill we could see column after column of [Confederate] troops coming to the rescue." This unnerved Crook to the point that he pleaded with Wright to withdraw Thoburn's command to the river's eastern shore. "When the enemy's strength commenced developing," Crook explained, "I desired to withdraw my troops to our side of the river." Wright greeted Crook's request with an emphatic "no." With Gordon's division near Castleman's Ferry and Wharton's and Rodes's divisions moving toward Island Ford, Wright confronted the reality that Early was "there in full force." "Nevertheless," as one New Yorker explained, Wright seemed "determined to fight them."

Instead of permitting Crook to withdraw Thoburn, Wright directed Brig. Gen. James Ricketts to take his division to "cross the river and support" Thoburn's troops. Unfortunately for Thoburn's command, Ricketts never carried out Wright's order.

An 1845 graduate of the Virginia Military Institute, Brig. Gen. Gabriel Wharton commanded one of Early's divisions. On July 17, 1864, he wrote his wife, Nannie, that he thought Early's advance to Washington proved "very successful" and that it would "virtually" end fighting in the region. Wharton's observation proved premature. (phcw)

"Wholly Exposed"

CHAPTER FIVE

JULY 18, 1864
LATE AFTERNOON–EARLY EVENING

Shortly after Thoburn's command crossed the Shenandoah River at Island Ford some of the officers of the 18th Connecticut Infantry seemed in a state of disbelief. Unbelievably, Thoburn's tiny command stood on the Shenandoah River's western shore while the remainder of Wright's force rested on the opposite side. Fearful of the destruction Thoburn's brigades could endure, an unidentified officer in the 18th Connecticut vented his frustration to the commanding officer of the 4th West Virginia Infantry, Lt. Col. John Luther Vance. William Walker, the chaplain of the 18th Connecticut, reportedly heard one of the 18th's officers tell Vance "that if the rebels understood the situation, they would not be slow in improving it to drive our little force back into the river."

Thoburn also understood the potentially dire circumstances his command confronted. Unfortunately, he was powerless to do anything about it. The only action Thoburn could take was to position his regiments in as defensible a position as possible and direct his regimental commanders

Modern-day view from grounds of the abbey looking east toward the Shenandoah River. (jn)

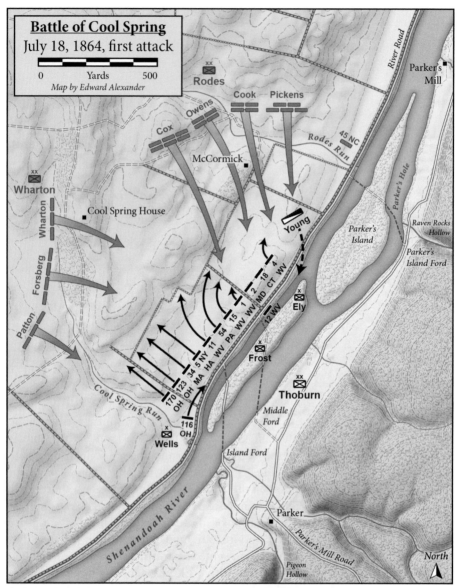

Battle of Cool Spring
July 18, 1864, first attack

0   Yards   500
Map by Edward Alexander

BATTLE OF COOL SPRING, JULY 18, 1864, FIRST ATTACK—While Confederates initially struck the southern end of the Union line, that assault was intended to distract attention away from a flank attack aimed at Thoburn's northern flank.

to send out "a strong skirmish line" to go "in search of the enemy." When the 116th Ohio's Col. James Washburn received instructions to deploy skirmishers, Washburn directed Lt. Col. Thomas Wildes to take four companies—B, C, D, and K—and locate the enemy. Union skirmishers, as Wildes recalled, "did not have to search . . . very long" for their foe.

Thoburn's skirmishers, according to some estimates, encountered "a heavy" Confederate "skirmish line" approximately half a mile from the river's edge. The Confederate skirmish line was so large that it overlapped Thoburn's line on both flanks. Troops from Gordon's division pressured the southern end of Thoburn's skirmish line, soldiers from Wharton's division advanced against the center, and skirmishers from Rodes's division targeted the northern flank. As the two skirmish lines engaged each other, Union batteries, most notably Lt. Jacob Lamb's Battery C, First Rhode Island Light Artillery, which took position on a ridge north of the Retreat, attempted to stymie the Confederate skirmishers. Although Union artillery would enjoy success later in the battle, its initial efforts to slow the Confederate onslaught proved futile and Thoburn's skirmishers retreated eastward.

The "heavy" Confederate "skirmish line" was only one of two challenges Thoburn confronted. As Gordon's, Wharton's, and Rodes's skirmishers attacked, Thoburn spied approximately 2,000 troops from Rodes's division approaching his northern flank. "A heavy force was moved forward upon my right flank, moving in two lines of battle at nearly right angles to our lines," Thoburn explained. With his skirmishers streaming toward the river and Rodes's division coming into view, Thoburn readied that portion of his command situated on the upland ridge, approximately seventy-five yards from the river's western shore, to meet the attack. Thoburn ordered his second brigade, which consisted of troops from West Virginia, Connecticut, and Maryland, to "change its front to the right to meet this attack." The brigade acted quickly, and in Thoburn's estimation "gallantly," to reposition itself to confront Rodes's regiments. Although able to present a front to Rodes's assault, the brigade confronted multiple challenges.

First, the reorientation of the command from facing west to north meant that Confederate skirmishers posted on the ridges west of Thoburn's line on the upland ridge could wreak havoc on

Surgeon John T. Nagle. After the war, Nagle became a strong advocate for pension rights of those who served as assistant surgeons during the Civil War. (jtn)

the brigade's left flank. Thoburn recalled that "the sharp enfilading fire from skirmishers and sharpshooters upon the high ground in front caused some unsteadiness" among the brigade. The situation became further exacerbated when the units on Thoburn's right flank, Lt. Col. John Vance's 4th West Virginia and Col. Samuel Young's provisional brigade of dismounted cavalry, struggled to slow the attack.

When Rodes's troops emerged from a grove of oak trees into a clearing on Thoburn's right flank, soldiers in Young's hodge-podge command could not believe their eyes. Private Charles McCoy, a sixteen-year-old from Bangor, Maine, who had enlisted in the 1st Maine Cavalry in January, noted simply that Rodes's division "advanced from out of the woods in our front." Although those who served in Young's command had experienced combat before, they had never experienced it as members of this provisional brigade which was asked to fight as infantry. Assembled thirteen days earlier at Camp Stoneman, a camp for dismounted cavalry located south of Washington, DC at Giesboro Point, Young's command (which drew together approximately 1,000 troopers from twenty-seven different cavalry regiments) never had an opportunity to appropriately prepare for combat as foot soldiers. These troopers, unfamiliar with infantry drill, were also required to carry muskets instead of the breechloading carbines to which they were accustomed. Decades after the conflict Pvt. McCoy enumerated the various difficulties Young's command confronted before the battle even started: "There were several reasons why we could not . . . fight. At Camp Stoneman those who had carbines had to give them up, and we were armed as infantry, and this, with the hard marching, carrying blankets and rations (if we had any), besides being mixed together, as we were, without organization, was enough to take the fight out of the best troops in the world."

Some in Young's brigade seemed keenly aware that the unit lacked cohesiveness and might not be able to effectively resist Rodes's assault. Surgeon John T. Nagle, who served as the chief medical officer of the dismounted cavalry, was among those who harbored such pessimism. Characterized by Col. Young as "always present and energetic in the discharge" of his "duties," Nagle conferred with other surgeons in Thoburn's command after the battle, began "to discuss the action they ought to take, if defeated in this engagement." It seemed "evident" to Nagle, with a heavy line of Confederate skirmishers to Thoburn's front and Rodes's Division moving against the northern flank, "that the small Union force that was engaged in this battle could not cope successfully with the larger attacking force of the enemy."

In "a clump of trees to the right of the dismounted cavalry," the surgeons conferred as to whether or not they should remain to take care of the wounded if the Confederates forced Thoburn to withdraw. Some determined they would stay only as long as their regiments remained. When their regiments withdrew, they would leave for the Shenandoah's opposite shore, leaving any wounded troops behind. Others believed their duty as surgeons required them to stay and treat the wounded even if that meant risking capture. The surgeons who favored remaining to care for the wounded understood that while this involved some risk, they believed it the lesser of two evils. Retreat, if it came, involved the risk of being shot in the back while crossing to the Shenandoah River's eastern side.

"The Surgeons consulted with each other with regard to the advisability of retreating with the army, and running the risk of being shot while slowly crossing," Nagle wrote. "Some concluded to stay and surrender," Nagle recalled, "others thought that they would sooner take the chances and dangers and being shot in crossing . . . than to be taken prisoners and sent, perhaps, to Libby for an indefinite period." Nagle trembled at the thought of being captured and Confederates stealing his personal possessions. "I concluded that the Confederates might make a considerable haul if they searched me," Nagle wrote.

As the surgeons contemplated what they would do, General William Cox's brigade of North Carolinians, positioned on the right of Rodes's line, approached Thoburn's skirmishers. Colonel Edwin Augustus Osborne, 4th North Carolina Infantry, recalled that as Cox's brigade passed through a body of woods and moved down the sloping terrain they saw an unmanned stone fence running perpendicular to Thoburn's line. Believing that whoever held this wall first possessed a

Colonel Edwin Osborne, 4th North Carolina Infantry, attended Statesville Military Academy in North Carolina before the Civil War. Osborne was wounded several times during the conflict, including at Seven Pines, Sharpsburg, and Spotsylvania. After the conflict, Osborne pursued various ventures, including teaching and the study of law. In 1881 he was ordained a priest in the Episcopal Church. (wcnc)

decided advantage, the North Carolinians hastened for it. "About half way between the two lines, in the valley, was a stone fence. As soon as this was seen our men made a dash for it," Osborne recalled.

While neither Thoburn nor his skirmishers paid attention to the wall as an important defensive feature on the landscape as they established lines that afternoon, the scene of Cox's men running for the wall alerted them to its importance and so they attempted to outrun the North Carolinians. "The Federals seeing this, and knowing the value of such a defence," Col. Osborne recalled, "made a dash for it at the same time. Away went both lines of battle at full speed as fast as their feet would carry them . . . both lines running for dear life to gain this coveted prize." The nature of the landscape afforded the North Carolinians an advantage. Cox's regiments raced to the wall running downhill, while Thoburn's skirmishers moved uphill at the double-quick. "Our men had the advantage of down grade, and gained the wall," observed an officer in the 4th North Carolina. In Col. Osborne's estimation Thoburn's skirmishers, which he believed "in much disorder," stood approximately fifty yards away from the wall at the moment the North Carolinians seized it.

Closer to the river, on Rodes's left flank, troops from General Phillip Cook's brigade of Georgians and Col. Samuel Pickens's brigade of Alabamians advanced toward Thoburn's northern flank protected by Young's dismounted brigade. As the Confederates, according to Capt. Robert E. Park, 12th Alabama Infantry, "halted on a little eminence, peppering them with bullets," a majority of troops in Young's command believed it folly to remain. One veteran wrote that some of Young's troopers, so unnerved by the sight, fled across the Shenandoah River to its eastern side "without firing a shot." A soldier in Young's brigade noted that the troops broke "in great disorder" and retreated "across the river."

While fear might have prompted some in Young's brigade to have fled quickly and not fire, the lack of volleys from Young's dismounted troopers was also a product of inadequate training. Armed with muskets instead of carbines, Sgt. James Henry Avery, 5th Michigan Cavalry, noted that with little training and combat experience with a musket, Young's brigade confronted a bevy of issues as they navigated the nine-step process to load and fire. Instead of tearing the cartridge and separating the bullet from the powder, pouring the powder into the musket barrel, seating the bullet, and then ramming the bullet, Sgt. Avery confessed to his diary that he rammed the entire cartridge. Since the paper that wrapped the cartridge was non-combustible, Avery could not discharge his musket. Patiently, Avery attached a ball-puller to the end of his ramrod and removed the bullet. "My old musket bothered me terribly in this fight; it would not go off as I had forgot to bite the cartridge, so I drew the ball," Avery wrote after the battle. Avery's problems did not end there. After he extracted the bullet, he leaned his ramrod against a tree, and then fell back closer to the river. When he went to load his musket again he realized his mistake and picked up another musket. "I . . . set my ramrod beside a tree. . . . To remedy this evil, I picked up a gun that was in order, as my gun was of no use without a rod," Avery explained.

Despite the various challenges that Young's dismounted brigade confronted, the conduct of his troops mortified Young. Remembered "as brave a man as ever straddled a horse," Young tried desperately to rally his command "on the bank of the river." While Young's attempt to stem the panic among his men largely proved futile, some remained and fought, among them Pvt. William H. Cushman.

A railroad conductor from Cleveland, Ohio, Cushman enlisted in the 2nd Ohio Cavalry on August 24, 1861. As the bulk of Young's command broke for the Shenandoah River, Cushman along with others from Young's command took cover "behind a fence, partially made of stone and rails" which lined the Shenandoah River's western bank. Second Lieutenant George Byard recalled that those from Young's command who remained laid on the ground and fired at their attackers through gaps in the fence. Unluckily for Cushman a Confederate bullet passed through one of those gaps, struck him in the head, and killed him instantly. Byard wrote to Cushman's widow, Mary: "We were laying on the ground firing. The ball that hit your husband passed between two rails [and] entered his head just above the right eye

Private William Cushman was initially buried on the battlefield. After the conflict, his remains were moved to the Winchester National Cemetery, grave 692. (jn)

passing entirely through the head." In an effort to console Cushman's grieving wife and six-year-old son William, Byard branded Cushman "a good soldier and a lover of man" and hoped that she and her son would take comfort "to know that your husband fell in a good cause facing the enemy of his country." Comrades buried Cushman on the western bank of the Shenandoah River. He remained interred there until after the conflict when his remains were removed to grave 792 in the Winchester National Cemetery.

Private William Wright, a native of Waupaca County, Wisconsin, who mustered into the 5th United States Cavalry on March 11, 1864, also took cover behind the makeshift barricade. Unable to fire effectively between openings in the fence, Wright ill-advisedly decided to "raise" himself to fire at troops in Rodes's division. Private Anthony W. Stumpe, who also served in the 5th United States Cavalry, was near Wright at the moment he raised himself up beyond the fence "to shoot." Before Wright fired, a Confederate bullet struck him in the head. Stumpe explained to Wright's widow, Mary: "I saw him raise to shoot when the fatal bullet took him in the head and caused his instant death." Regarded as "a good soldier and gentleman, as well as a good Christian," Stumpe expressed to Wright's widow and three children his "hope" that Wright "is in a better World than this."

Despite Young's effort to rally his command and the resolve of some to remain and fight, once the lion's share of Young's brigade broke "in great disorder" and retreated "across the river" the burden of protecting Thoburn's northern flank against Rodes's assault shifted to Lt. Col. John L. Vance's 4th West Virginia Infantry. While enlistments for some in Vance's command expired by July 18 and a portion of the regiment carried discharge papers in their pockets, not one of those veterans who had fulfilled their commitment were technically required to fight, but their sense of responsibility to their comrades and the Union prevented them from sitting out. "The Fourth boys being plucky fellows generally, these discharged men said that they would not stand back while their comrades were going into a fight," one West Virginian recalled.

With the bulk of Young's command hastening for the Shenandoah's eastern shore, Vance immediately recognized the threat his regiment confronted. Vance, whose regiment had been rushed to Thoburn's northern flank at "the double quick" the moment Union and Confederate skirmishers engaged, took two companies, as a veteran of the regiment recalled, "to protect our flank . . . left wholly exposed." The difficulty Vance's regiment confronted was that troops from Rodes's division had the protection of the stone wall which ran perpendicular to Thoburn's line. "From this point they poured upon us a terrible enfilading fire," recalled a veteran of the regiment. As much as Vance's command attempted to hold their position, the effort proved futile. Vance had no other alternative but to withdraw his men to Thoburn's second line, a stonewall-lined road which ran along the Shenandoah's River's western bank. "Col. Vance seeing there was no other alternative, gave the command to fall back, whereupon they fell back in some haste to a stone fence some fifty yards in our rear and immediately upon the river bank," recalled a veteran in the regiment.

When Vance withdrew his regiment to Thoburn's line along the river, it exposed Col. William Ely's 18th Connecticut. Ely noted that when "the enemy enfiladed and drove" Vance's "command from the lot" his flank was now "unprotected." Ely attempted

Born in Killingly, Connecticut, Col. William Ely attended Brown University. Ely was commissioned colonel of the 18th Connecticut Infantry in August 1862. He was captured at the Second Battle of Winchester in June 1863. He was paroled on March 22, 1864, and returned to his regiment. He died in 1906. (jn)

to reposition his command to meet the threats to his front and flanks. That task proved difficult as Ely realized that repositioning portions of his regiment would make them vulnerable not only to fire from Rodes's brigades, but potentially from Union troops posted in Thoburn's second line behind the stone wall along the river's bank. "I changed direction to the rear on tenth company to avoid being enfiladed. I could not then change front forward," Ely explained the day after the battle, "because it would have thrown my command into the fire of our own troops, which had just been stationed behind the stone wall on our left."

As the pressure mounted against the northern portion of the Union line, Thoburn quickly repositioned portions of his command to meet the threat. First, Thoburn directed Col. Daniel Frost, commanding the third brigade, "to oblique his first line to the right and present a front to the advancing foe." Initially it seemed that the repositioning of Frost's regiments slowed the Confederate attack. Lieutenant Colonel John Linton, 54th Pennsylvania, wrote of this initial success: "The enemy attacked the right of the line . . . their line being formed at an oblique angle with the river. To meet this advance a change of front of the left of our line was ordered, which was gallantly executed under fire and the enemy for a time being repulsed." Unfortunately for Frost's brigade, the advantage proved short-lived. Repositioning his command from facing west to facing north meant that Frost's brigade would be susceptible to fire not only from Rodes's division, but from Wharton's troops on the upland ridge. From that point Wharton's command would be able to fire into Frost's left flank. Confederate troops on Wharton's right flank would be in position to fire into Frost's rear. When Lt. Col. Edward Murray, 5th New York Heavy Artillery, spied Frost's vulnerability, he ordered his New Yorkers to attack Wharton's troops.

Murray's attack, while it might have momentarily protected Frost's left flank, came at a high cost. Thirty-three percent of the Union soldiers killed at the battle came from the 5th New York Heavy Artillery—the highest death rate among all of Thoburn's regiments. Among those who perished was Pvt. James Darrah. An immigrant from Manchester, England, Darrah, along with his wife Amy and daughter Minnie, lived in Springfield, Massachusetts prior to the conflict. One week after the battle, Pvt. Jacob A. Blackmon wrote Darrah's widow with the grim news. Blackmon, who confessed that the death of such an "esteemed . . . honorable patriot [and] companion in arms . . . could hardly grieve me more were it a near and dear relative," explained that Darrah "was shot through the head . . . and killed instantly."

While Darrah's widow and child sought a way to survive, the burden of widowhood and raising children proved too much for some. Margaret Burns, widowed after her husband Pvt. James Burns, 5th New York Heavy Artillery, perished at Cool Spring, struggled to make ends meet. Less than one year after Pvt. Burns's death, Margaret, unable to care for her two children, seven-year-old William and five-year-old Susan, decided to "abandon" them and pass guardianship to James Reiley.

Lieutenant Colonel Murray, although he survived the assault against Wharton's troops, suffered two wounds. As Murray led his New Yorkers forward a bullet struck him in the right wrist. The wound "bled profusely and to such an extent that he fainted from the loss of blood." As a contingent of soldiers attempted to evacuate Murray from the battlefield "he received a gunshot wound in the back and over the region of the kidneys." At this moment panic seized the New Yorkers. They abandoned their position, and Murray, on the battlefield.

As the 5th New York Heavy Artillery broke, Frost's left flank once again became vulnerable. The situation became exacerbated when a bullet tore through Frost's abdomen. Frost immediately recognized the seriousness of his wound "and pronounced" it "to be mortal." Perhaps concerned about falling into enemy hands, Frost kicked his spurs into his horse and headed for the opposite bank of the Shenandoah River. According to Lt. Col. Van Hartness Bukey, 11th West Virginia Infantry, Frost remained alert enough to converse with various officers, including his adjutant general, "giving him directions what to do with his official papers and private effects." Once on the Shenandoah River's eastern shore, Frost rode to the home of Eben Jenkins, a farmer at Castleman's Ferry.

Born in Ireland in 1828, Lt. Col. Edward Murray, received multiple wounds at Cool Spring and was captured. Murray received a promotion to brevet brigadier general in March 1865. After the conflict, he lived in New York City. The wounds he received at Cool Spring plagued him for the rest of his life. He died in 1876. (ahec)

Lieutenant Colonel Thomas Morris, 15th West Virginia Infantry, was killed at Cool Spring. When Morris's friends in Cameron, West Virginia, learned of his death they gathered Cameron's citizens to offer a resolution in Morris's honor. The resolution praised Morris as one of the community's "best and most useful citizens . . . a brave man." (rw)

There, in Bukey's estimation, Frost "was kindly cared for and had every possible attention which the place afforded." Frost died that night at 10:50 p.m. His remains were sent home to Wheeling, West Virginia, and interred in Mount Wood Cemetery eight days after the battle.

The collapse of the 5th New York Heavy Artillery, Frost's wounding, and the fate of other officers in Frost's brigade—such as Lt. Col. Thomas Morris, 15th West Virginia Infantry, who was killed during the fight—sent shock waves throughout Frost's brigade, who abandoned their position and broke for the Shenandoah River. All of these factors, recorded a member of Frost's command, "resulted in the discomfiture of our troops, who were forced back over the river." Eleven days after the battle, Thoburn concluded that, after Frost's mortal wounding, the brigade "was thrown into some confusion."

With Frost's brigade and Murray's New Yorkers retreating for the Shenandoah River, any hope that Col. Ely had of maintaining Thoburn's first line vanished. Ely explained the day after the battle: "Suddenly several large regiments on our left broke and dashed into the river, and the rebel fire became more concentrated each moment." Ely, "seeing no colors in the open field except my own," ordered the 18th Connecticut "to fall back" to Thoburn's second line. While some in the 18th Connecticut took position behind the stone wall which lined the river's western shore, some of Ely's troops thought it folly to remain and retreated to the Shenandoah River's eastern side. That experience of retreating from Thoburn's first line to the stone wall and beyond proved difficult for a variety of reasons.

First, retreating troops believed that as they withdrew eastward, Confederates fired explosive bullets at them. On the evening of July 18, Cpl. Charles Lynch, 18th Connecticut Infantry, wrote in his diary: "In this battle it was claimed the rebs used explosive bullets on us. . . . As I made my way almost to the top of the [eastern] bank, pulling myself up by the bushes, an explosive bullet struck near me." Unnerved by the experience, Lynch recorded that "the report and the fire from it cause me to loose my hold on the bushes and slip down the bank into the river."

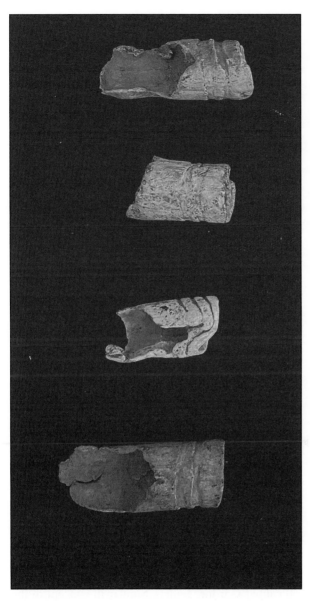

Defective Confederate Gardner bullets uncovered at Cool Spring. A number of these, along with other artifacts unearthed at Cool Spring, are part of an exhibition about the battle in the Lodge at Shenandoah University's River Campus at Cool Spring Battlefield. (mcwi)

Despite Lynch's claim, and the reality that two types of explosive bullets existed during the conflict—Samuel Gardiner's "Musket Shell," a bullet manufactured out of pewter which contained a copper fuse in the bullet's base which exploded the bullet approximately 2.5 seconds after it was fired, and Reuben Shaler's Patent Sectional Bullet, a lead bullet consisting of three stacked cones which separated after firing—archaeological investigations at Cool Spring over the past half century cast serious doubt as

The swirling waters of Parker's Hole was an obstacle that retreating Union soldiers did not anticipate. (jn)

to the validity of Lynch's claim. More than likely what Lynch believed to be explosive bullets were defective .58 caliber Gardner bullets. Similar in concept to the .58 caliber Minié ball, Gardner bullets were plagued with production flaws, the most significant of which were air pockets in the bullet. The air pockets weakened the bullet's structural integrity and when fired the bullet blew apart, mimicking an exploding bullet. Various archaeological works at Cool Spring since the 1980s have uncovered significant numbers of Gardner bullets which exploded as a result of air pockets.

Additionally, Union soldiers retreating to the Shenandoah's eastern side also contended with the

Shenandoah River. While easily crossed at most points, some soldiers were unaware of Parker's Hole—a deep abyss amid the Shenandoah's otherwise fordable waters that proved a deadly obstacle. "It was a fearful thing to re-cross that river, as it was deep in places," explained Cpl. Charles Lynch. Sergeant Thomas J. Aldrich was among those from the 18th Connecticut who drowned. "The fording was exceedingly difficult," explained the 18th Connecticut's chaplain, "and in the hurry of the moment many of the men rushed into the river regardless of the depth of the water, when in many cases the boys had to swim for their life, and quite a number struggled in vain, and at length found a watery grave."

Some fell victim to enemy bullets while in the river, among them Pvt. James M. Smith, 18th Connecticut Infantry. A farmer from Killingly, Connecticut, a bullet struck James and knocked him down into the water. His brother Samuel stood behind him at the moment James was struck. As the Shenandoah's current carried James north, Samuel confronted an unimaginable situation—attempt to save his brother and risk death, or continue across to the river's eastern bank. Samuel chose the latter. James's body floated several miles downstream and was pulled out of the river by a local resident and buried in a temporary grave. Haunted by the scene, Samuel returned to the battlefield in the spring of 1865, once the conflict ended in Virginia, to find his brother's remains. On April 9, 1865, Samuel penned his wife from Harpers Ferry: "My 4 months pay I shall keep a while so that if there is any chance to get poor Jimmy's body, I may have some by me to work with." Samuel found his brother's grave, had his remains removed, and then buried in the Smith family cemetery in East Killingly, Connecticut.

The scene of retreating soldiers being shot while in the river and then drowning haunted Union surgeon John T. Nagle. Nearly three decades after the battle Nagle recalled that "there were also a number shot and drowned while crossing the river. I shall always

One could only imagine the thoughts that coursed through the mind of Pvt. Samuel Smith (right) as he saw his brother Pvt. James Smith (left) shot in the back and swept away by the river's current. (ms)

Colonel James Washburn, 116th Ohio Infantry, believed the wound he received at Cool Spring mortal. Remarkably Washburn survived. After the war, Washburn moved with his wife, Mariah, to Rockbridge, Wisconsin. Washburn pursued various political ventures including one term in the state assembly. He died in 1898.
(mcwi)

remember the piercing shriek of one poor fellow who successfully crossed the river and was climbing up the bank ahead of me and in my range . . . when a Confederate bullet struck him, and he fell back into the river, and was seen by me no more."

As portions of his command disintegrated and "fled ingloriously across the river," Thoburn, who remained, in the estimation of one Ohio officer, "the coolest man on the field," shuffled the regiments that remained to the meet various threats, the most significant of which was pressure on the Union line's northern flank. Thoburn moved Col. James Washburn's 116th Ohio and Capt. John W. Chamberlin's 123rd Ohio, initially posted on southern flank, to the Union line's northern end. As the Buckeyes arrived they saw, in the words of one of the 116th Ohio's veterans, "a large body of rebels . . . bearing down heavily on the right . . . and the gallant 4th West Virginia fighting to maintain its position against desperate odds."

At the moment the Buckeyes reached Thoburn's right flank, a bullet, presumably from Col. Samuel Pickens's Alabamians, pierced Washburn's left eye. The bullet exited Washburn's head below the right ear. News of Washburn's severe wound sent shockwaves throughout the regiment. "Sincerely loved" by his men, everyone in the regiment, including Washburn, believed the wound mortal. "He was struck by a minnie ball at very close range, and the wound was a frightful one," recalled Lt. Col. Thomas Wildes, who assumed command of the regiment. A contingent of Buckeyes carried Washburn across the Shenandoah River to its eastern side where surgeons, after they examined his wound, "could give no hope of his recovery." Hopeless, Washburn directed that his "sword and belt, watch, pocket-book, papers, letters and other small articles . . . be sent to his family."

News of Washburn's wound demoralized the 116th Ohio. Wildes recalled that men were "shedding tears" after learning of Washburn's wound. Corporal John Mitchell wrote despondently: "Washburn supposed to be killed."

Remarkably, Washburn survived his wound. Sent to Harpers Ferry, Washburn recovered sufficiently to visit the regiment in its camps along the banks of Cedar Creek, south of Middletown, Virginia, on October 26.

Although he recovered adequately enough to spend time with his regiment and later assume command of forces at Wheeling, West Virginia, Washburn dealt with the pain of that wound for the remainder of his life.

In addition to the loss of his left eye Washburn experienced, as one newspaper correspondent reported, "lasting effects . . . partial paralysis of one side of his face, partial loss of speech and a general breakdown of his constitution." Despite the agony he endured for the remainder of his life, Washburn refused to let it deter him from pursuing various endeavors, including political office. Washburn held a number of elected positions in Wisconsin after the conflict (Washburn and his wife Mariah moved to Rockbridge, Wisconsin, in 1868). In addition to serving in a variety of posts in Richland County, Wisconsin, including chairman of the county board of supervisors, Washburn served one term in the Wisconsin State Assembly. He died on May 12, 1898, from "disease of the heart and lungs, which was followed by disease of the kidneys."

Despite the demoralizing impact of Washburn's wound, Wildes wasted no time in determining how best to bolster Thoburn's northern flank. Wildes believed the most vulnerable part of Thoburn's defense was the area between the stone wall and the river's western bank. Immediately, he ordered Capt. Thornton Mallory to take two companies and throw "up a breastwork of stones and logs across this space." As Mallory's companies rushed to the scene, erected breastworks, and "opened a deadly fire upon" the Confederates who attempted to exploit the gap (Pickens's Alabamians), Union soldiers who watched Mallory's companies stood in awe of their bravery. A veteran of the 4th West Virginia, the regiment that immediately benefited from the 116th's efforts, explained in a letter home the day after the battle: "The 116th Ohio . . . came to our assistance. . . . [L]et me in praise of the 116th say that better soldiers are no where to be found."

Shortly after Mallory secured the gap "between the wall and the river" Wildes ordered Sgt. Silas King, with ten men from Company F, "further to the right" to secure the southern side of a "stone wall running at right angles" with the stone wall behind which Thoburn's main line rested. The combat proved intense

Brigadier General James Ricketts. For decades after the battle, veterans in Thoburn's command pondered how the battle might have fared had Ricketts's division crossed the Shenandoah River. (loc)

The artillery support Col. Charles H. Tompkins's batteries provided to Thoburn's troops proved critical to averting disaster at Cool Spring. (jrb)

as troops from Rodes's command positioned on the northern side of the wall and King's detachment fired at point blank range. King's contingent succeeded in its mission. "The gallant sergeant and his men," Wildes wrote, "after a hot contest, cleared the rebels out from behind this wall, killing and wounding some of them almost within the length of some of their guns, the other side of the river wall." In awe of King's bravery, Wildes penned in praise: "He exhibited ability to command and determination and daring bravery not often met with in the rank and file."

The 116th Ohio's efforts proved a critical moment in the fight. Wildes's ability to identify vulnerable points and strengthen them proved critical to the security of Thoburn's line, which hugged the Shenandoah's western shore. Still, Thoburn's men hoped that the support promised them earlier in the afternoon, Ricketts's division, would arrive.

As the battle raged on the west side of the Shenandoah River, General Ricketts led his division down the mountain, across Judge Parker's Retreat, and toward Island Ford. Confederates spied the advance. Chaplain James Sheeran recalled that the "well dressed" division with "their numerous battle flags waving with seeming triumph . . . present a grand and formidable appearance, as they move in solid column to the bank of the Shenandoah." When Ricketts's column came into view of Capt. George Chapman's Monroe Battery, Chapman directed two twenty-pound Parrott Rifles to shell the advancing column.

General Wright, who accompanied Ricketts's division, turned to Col. Charles H. Tompkins, the VI Corps artillery chief, to silence Chapman. Quickly, Tompkins ordered Batteries C and G, 1st Rhode Island Light Artillery, into the bluffs on the Shenandoah's eastern side and to form on the flanks of Battery E, 1st West Virginia Artillery, which had supported Thoburn since he crossed the Shenandoah River. [The four ten-pound Parrott rifles of Battery C took position north of the West Virginians. Battery G situated its four ordnance rifles south of Battery E. In addition to silencing Chapman's twenty-pound Parrott rifles, Tompkins directed his guns at the Confederates attacking Thoburn's position.

Firing at the attacking Confederate infantry brigades arguably proved the more difficult of the two tasks. With troops from Rodes's Division in such close proximity to Thoburn's line along the river's edge, Tompkins hoped to avoid inflicting "friendly fire" on Thoburn's troops. "The lines were so close to each other," Wildes recalled. Despite "some damage" to Thoburn's troops, the artillery fire from the bluffs created the desired impact. A newspaper correspondent near Capt. George Adams's Battery G, 1st Rhode Island Light Artillery, wrote: "At this critical moment, Adams' Rhode Island Battery came into position on an eminence overlooking the valley

Modern-day view near position occupied by Battery C, 1st Rhode Island Light Artillery. (jn)

Captain George Adams, born in Providence, Rhode Island in 1834, received his commission as captain of Battery G, 1st Rhode Island Light Artillery, on January 30, 1863. Adams received three brevet promotions for gallantry on the battlefield. Adams was highly regarded, as one chronicler noted in 1867, for his "distinguished reputation for knowledge of his profession, military skill, and great personal bravery." (jrb)

below. They immediately opened upon the enemy with shot and shell . . . creating great havoc among them. The range was very accurate and each shell burst in their midst."

As Tompkins's cannon wreaked havoc on Rodes's command, Chapman's two twenty-pound Parrott rifles attempted to silence them, but to no avail. "The enemy finding the damage to their infantry so great, attempted to silence the battery firing upon them with twenty pound Parrotts, which, however, lasted but a moment, as they in turn were fired upon and forced to cease," reported a correspondent attached to Battery G. Although Chapman's Parrott rifles could not dislodge the Union batteries in the bluffs, Confederate cannon did inflict some damage to infantry regiments positioned behind the batteries in support. Surgeon Daniel M. Holt, 121st New York Infantry, saw three soldiers from a New Jersey regiment killed and at least six others in another New Jersey regiment supporting one of the Rhode Island batteries struck by shrapnel from Confederate artillery. Sergeant John Hartwell, 121st New York, recalled that shells from Chapman's guns sailed over the Union batteries but "exploded in the ranks of our troops laying in the rear."

As events unfolded rapidly late that afternoon and into early evening, General Crook accompanied General Ricketts to the banks of the Shenandoah River to find a suitable location for Ricketts to cross and lend critical support to Thoburn's beleaguered brigades. However, after seeing the great strength of the Confederate assault and the scene of Union soldiers retreating, Ricketts, as Crook explained eleven days after the battle, "did not think it prudent under the circumstances to cross his men." Incensed over Ricketts's unwillingness to cross, Crook sought Wright's intercession. Unfortunately for Crook and Thoburn, Wright agreed with Ricketts's assessment. Despite his earlier promise to support Thoburn, Wright too believed that crossing would only needlessly sacrifice Ricketts's troops in a battle that appeared lost. "Gen. Ricketts declined to go to their support, and allowed many of my men to be sacrificed. I lost some valuable men here, murdered by incompetency or worse. I reported the facts to Gen. Wright, but that was the end of it," explained an enraged Crook.

The lack of support from Ricketts also incensed and dumbfounded Thoburn's troops who could see, as a surgeon in Thoburn's command explained, "on the opposite side of the river" Ricketts's troops "quietly resting and . . . apparently oblivious of the battle that was passing. . . . It seemed strange to us . . . that we received no support whatever from the main army."

Although Ricketts did not cross, the stubborn defense of Thoburn's remaining regiments, coupled with artillery support, forced Rodes to halt, pull back closer to the ridge in front of Thoburn's position, and regroup in preparation for another attack. A soldier in the 12th West Virginia Infantry wrote days after the battle that he was delighted to see the Confederates "about charge." However, delight turned to dread as the West Virginian spied Rodes's brigades preparing to "re shout and re-charge."

"The Advantage of Position"

CHAPTER SIX
JULY 18, 1864
EARLY EVENING NIGHTTIME

As troops from Thoburn's command and Ricketts's division mingled with each other on this ground—owned by Shenandoah University—on the east side of the Shenandoah River on the night of July 18, troops from Ricketts's command informed Thoburn's troops that they wanted to cross the Shenandoah and come to their aid, but that Ricketts would not permit it. (jn)

As Thoburn's troops hunkered down in position along the Shenandoah River's western edge and Rodes's brigades regrouped, Thoburn, despite all that his command confronted, believed his position a strong one. Archaeological investigations conducted at the battlefield in 1994, led by Joseph W. A. Whitehorne and Clarence Geier, revealed that the road in which Thoburn's final defensive line rested did not sit at the edge of the floodplain, but instead was cut into the river's bank. This meant that the road Thoburn's infantry occupied, approximately twenty feet wide, sat anywhere from six to fifteen feet below the stone wall shielding Thoburn's command. He wrote of the position's strength: "The men were protected by the embankment of a road that ran along the river bank and under a large bluff." Thoburn, and his subordinates, believed that, with the advantages the position offered, it would be foolhardy to retreat across to the Shenandoah's eastern shore until darkness draped the battlefield. "We dare not retreat, however,

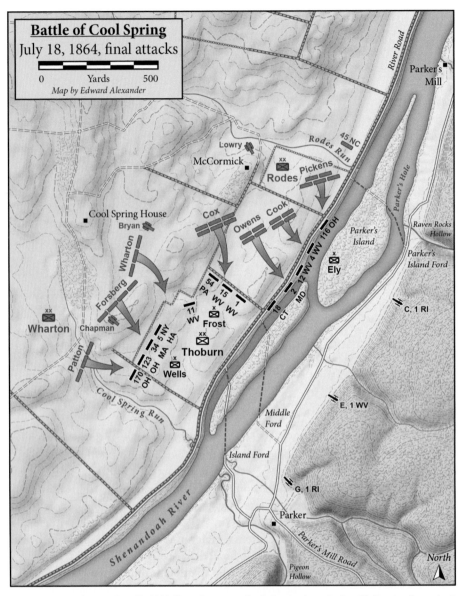

Battle of Cool Spring
July 18, 1864, final attacks

0   Yards   500

Map by Edward Alexander

BATTLE OF COOL SPRING, JULY 18, 1864, FINAL ATTACKS—Confederates launched multiple assaults against the Union line after Thoburn reformed it in the roadbed that paralleled the Shenandoah River's western bank. The strength of the position, coupled with support from Union artillery in the bluffs on the opposite shore, prevented Thoburn's destruction.

as long as that rebel line lay in our front, unless under cover of darkness," Lt. Col. Wildes explained.

Rodes's regiments too learned of the position's advantages as they neared it during their final assault. Captain Matt Manly, 2nd North Carolina Infantry, wrote simply: "The enemy had the advantage of position after we had driven him back" toward the river. Captain Robert E. Park, 12th Alabama Infantry, explained in his diary: "A large number remained concealed near the river at the foot of the hill, and did some execution, firing at our men as they exposed themselves." As Confederates reached within fifty yards of the stone wall, Thoburn's infantry delivered volleys which stymied the final Confederate assault. An infantryman in the 12th West Virginia wrote three days after the battle that when Rodes's regiments neared the stone wall Thoburn's troops "sweetened" their foe "with sugar of lead." Additionally, the Union batteries in the bluffs continued to wreak havoc. Brothers James and Jacob Teachey, natives of Duplin County, North Carolina, who served in the 30th North Carolina, were struck by artillery shells. James was killed instantly while his brother Jacob, struck in the bowels by shrapnel, lingered for months after the battle. Jacob succumbed to his wounds on January 17, 1865.

The strength of Thoburn's position coupled with the destructive fire from the federal batteries in the bluffs compelled Rodes to refocus his priorities as the sun began to set. The focus could no longer be on destroying Union forces on the Shenandoah's western shore, but protecting his troops from Union artillery on the other side. Although not yet ready to quit the battlefield, Rodes ordered his troops to withdraw to the reverse slope of the ridge in front of Thoburn's position, out of view of Union cannon. One by one Rodes's brigades disengaged and marched west. Unfortunately for the Confederates, as the brigades withdrew they did so piecemeal which at times, in the estimation of some Confederate officers, left other units vulnerable. For example, when Brig. Gen. William Cox's brigade withdrew, the brigade on Cox's left, Brig. Gen. Bryan Grimes's brigade, which at the battle of Cool Spring was commanded by Col. William Owens, had its right flank exposed. Colonel David Cowand, 32nd North Carolina Infantry, estimated that at the moment Cox's North Carolinians withdrew Owens's brigade stood "within thirty steps of the enemy's colors." Cowand complained that "when the troops on the right were ordered back" it "left our right so much exposed that we had to be swung back." During that movement a bullet from one of Thoburn's infantrymen struck

Born in Canada in 1834, Lt. Col. Thomas F. Wildes took command of the 116th Ohio after Colonel Washburn received his wound. In 1962 the town of Dayton, Virginia, erected a monument in Wildes's honor for the role he played in convincing Union general Philip H. Sheridan to not burn the community in retaliation for the killing of Sheridan's chief engineer 1st Lt. John R. Meigs on October 3, 1864. After the conflict, Wildes worked as an attorney in Akron, Ohio, and wrote a regimental history of the 116th Ohio. Wildes died in 1883. (np)

Owens in the bowels. An attorney from Mecklenburg, North Carolina, Owens had just returned to his regiment earlier that day after recovering from wounds he received to his middle finger and side two months earlier at the battle of Spotsylvania Courthouse. Owens died the following day. Initially, he was buried in the Old Chapel Cemetery in Millwood, Virginia. In March 1867 Owens's remains were moved and reinterred in the Old Settlers Cemetery in Charlotte, North Carolina.

As Rodes's brigades withdrew out of view of the Union artillery in the bluffs that evening, some of his veterans appeared frustrated. Despite initially driving Thoburn's command, as Pvt. George Nichols, 61st Georgia Infantry, explained, "back in great confusion," the Union batteries "playing" on their foe eliminated any hope, as the 32nd North Carolina's David Cowand lamented in his report of the battle, of capturing "a large number of prisoners." "We would have had no difficulty in capturing all the Yankees on this side of the river in a short time, but for the fact that the enemy . . . artillery, on the heights . . . was enabled to pour a deadly fire into our ranks with impunity," lamented the 4th North Carolina's John Alexander Stikeleather.

Throughout the evening and into night's darkness Confederate cannon from Lowry's, Bryan's, and Chapman's batteries attempted to dislodge the Union artillery. The spectacle of batteries dueling that night left some in awe. "It was now fully dark, and the scene was beautiful," wrote Sgt. Milton Humphreys, a member of Bryan's battery. "From the flash of the guns we could see the shell coming like a meteor, and then came the noise of the shell, and lastly the report of the guns," Humphreys explained. The Confederate battery commanders quickly realized the futility of trying to dislodge the Union cannons from their commanding position. Sergeant Humphreys noted that each cannon fired "six rounds" and then "retired . . . and went into park under cover of a forest from the enemy's guns on the mountain."

Despite not being able to inflict any damage on the Union batteries in the bluffs and drive them from the commanding position, the fire from Confederate cannon inflicted some casualties among troops in Ricketts's division, as an officer in the 4th New Jersey

Infantry recalled, which was "forming near the Shenandoah about dark." The chaplain of the 15th New Jersey Infantry recalled that a shell landed among the 10th New Jersey and seriously wounded Capt. George Scott. The wound so severely disabled Scott that he was discharged from the regiment on October 19, 1864. In the 15th New Jersey, a round from a Confederate cannon struck Cpl. Watson Chambers in the knee. Chambers died three days later leaving behind his wife, Mary, and five-year-old son, Lorenzo. A Confederate shell burst in the ranks of the 4th New Jersey and mortally wounded Privates John Price and George Lee, both members of Company C. Price, according to his company commander, Capt. Caleb Wright, "was killed by the explosion of a shell thrown from the enemy, a piece of which struck him causing death in a few hours." Private Lee, "struck in the arm cutting the bone in two about the elbow joint," also received, according the 4th New Jersey's Capt. Robert S. Johnston, "severe cuts in his head, one in the chin, one on the left face & one directly under the left eye, all of them about two inches in length." Lee lingered until 4:00 p.m. the following day. Captain Johnston explained to Lee's father that after he "saw him breathe his last" men from the regiment fashioned "a box . . . for him" and buried "him between Snickers Gap and the Shenandoah River under a tree with a head board to mark the place . . . about one half mile from the Gap."

Once the Confederate batteries withdrew and it appeared that Early's divisions would not launch any additional assaults that night, Thoburn carried out General Crook's "order to fall back" to the Shenandoah's eastern side. Although Thoburn's troops were not "followed or fired upon" by Rodes's regiments as they recrossed the river, the potential certainly existed with the Confederates hunkered down behind the reverse slop of the ridge to Thoburn's front, a distance, as the 123rd Ohio's Capt. John W. Chamberlin estimated, was "only about 100 yards."

As Thoburn's regiments withdrew, efforts were made to evacuate as many of the wounded as possible. While Wildes boasted that the 116th Ohio "carried over all our wounded"—nine in total—not all regiments could safely evacuate their injured comrades from the battlefield. When the 123rd Ohio received orders to retreat to the river's opposite shore two members of the regiment noticed that Sgt. David D. Terry, a thirty-two-year old father of two boys, was stuck "in the corner of a fence about 20 feet in advance" of Thoburn's line, suffering from a bullet wound to his "left breast, just below the nipple." With Terry's "face to the enemy," two unidentified men from the regiment rescued him.

With Terry desperately clinging to life, the two Buckeyes carried their comrade to Parker's Island, the northernmost of two islands which sat midway between the Shenandoah River's eastern and western shores, and left him there. Whether Terry asked to be left on Parker's Island as the experience of being moved proved too painful or his comrades believed they could not perform the task without risking their own safety is unclear. Evidence indicates, however, that Terry was not the only wounded Union soldier left on Parker's Island. "He was carried by two men of our Regt. onto the island & left there with other wounded men, it being impossible at that time to take them any further," explained Chamberlin in a letter to Terry's wife three days after the battle.

In his final moments, it appeared that Terry turned his thoughts to his wife Mary and two sons, Joseph and Lycurgus. Resigned to his fate, Terry feared that the few possessions he carried, "his watch, pocket-book, knife, and all of his trinkets," might fall into enemy hands; he hid them, recalled one veteran of the regiment, "under a log by his side." 1st Lt. Charles M. Keyes wrote of Terry's final moments: "Knowing his hours were few, lying there alone, dying, with only God's Angels watching over him, his last thoughts were of dear ones at home, secreting his effects . . . hoping them to fall into the hands of his friends, that his wife and babies might receive this, his last, his dying gift . . . with the sad murmurings of the Shenandoah chanting its endless requiem." Two days after the battle, once Early's army marched west toward Winchester, Terry's comrades found his lifeless body and discovered what he had done. Chamberlin ordered Terry buried on Parker's Island. Unable to "procure any coffin" Chamberlin directed that Terry's body be wrapped "in a blanket" and a "board . . . with his name & regiment" be inscribed on it and placed at the head of the grave.

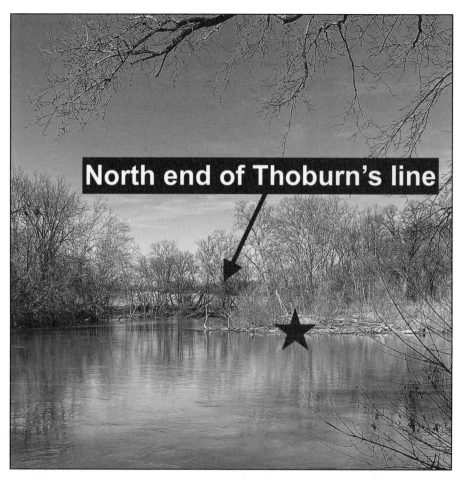

North end of Thoburn's line

Chamberlin, who confessed to Terry's wife Mary that he "felt his loss more deeply than that of any other man," clipped a lock of Terry's hair and sent it, along with all that Terry hid under the log, to Terry's widow, Mary. While Chamberlin admitted that "human sympathy avails little" he hoped that Mary, who received an $8 per month pension from the federal government, would find comfort that no one in the regiment "was a braver or truer soldier" than Terry, someone who "always knew his duty & performed it well . . . was always cool and collected, foremost in daring, and knew no such thing as fear."

Once Thoburn's troops withdrew to the opposite side of the river, Confederate sharpshooters moved closer to the river's edge. Meanwhile, two companies from the 37th Massachusetts and a contingent of forty infantrymen from the 2nd Rhode Island, armed

Modern-day view of the area between the two islands. The southern tip of Parker's Island is indicated on the image with a star. The gap between the islands shows Thoburn's northern flank. (jn)

Lieutenant Colonel George L. Montague, 37th Massachusetts, commanded the Union picket line on the night of July 18. At the war's outset, Montague served in the 6th Wisconsin Infantry. He received a commission as major of the 37th Massachusetts in August 1862. He was wounded at Spotsylvania on May 12, 1864. He died in 1912. (ahec)

with Spencer repeating rifles, took position along the river's eastern bank to protect against a Confederate crossing and also aid wounded Union soldiers to make it safely across the Shenandoah. Lt. Col. George Montague, 37th Massachusetts, who served as officer of the day and commanded the picket line along the Shenandoah, permitted some pickets to climb into the trees which lined the river's bank to maintain a close watch on Early's pickets.

Clear weather conditions, coupled with a nearly full moon (full moon was on July 19, 1864), afforded Montague's pickets in the trees an opportunity to view Confederates scouring the battlefield for their own wounded and prisoners of war. Shots pierced the air throughout the night. A veteran of the 37th Massachusetts recalled that "in the gloom of that July evening the first test of the Spencer rifles was made." The fire from one of Montague's men became so menacing that an unidentified member of the 4th North Carolina Infantry aimed to end it. While the unknown Tar Heel eventually "brought down" the Union picket who "annoyed," as the regiment's Col. Edwin A. Osborne recalled, "our men very much . . . firing from the tree-tops," other Union pickets saw the muzzle flash and "pierced" the North Carolinian "with bullets."

As the occasional crack of small arms fire pierced the nighttime air, Thoburn's veterans "lighted" fires "on the river bank," prepared "coffee the soldier's elixir of life," and attempted to make sense of what had happened—why ultimately seventy-two of their comrades had been killed or mortally wounded and another 301 wounded. Could the sacrifice have been avoided? Certainly the troops who fought into the night believed, as a veteran of the 18th Connecticut noted, "they did all that men could do in the circumstances in which they had been placed, and obeyed orders. . . . The result greatly disappointed the officers and men generally, and all felt mortified and chagrined at the result."

Arguably no one was more "mortified and chagrined" than the 18th's Col. William Ely. As he looked at what remained of his regiment that night— no more than sixty men—he burst into tears. An exceedingly frustrated Ely told his troops that evening: "Boys . . . I am willing to lead you against an equal, or even double your number of rebels, but this being shut up in a slaughter-pen I cannot stand." "Col. Ely and other officers of the regiment wept that night at the useless slaughter and broken up condition of the regiment," recalled the regiment's chaplain.

Despite the artillery support, Thoburn's veterans seemed mystified that Wright refused to send one solitary reinforcement to the Shenandoah's western side. "Why we were not supported in this engagement was . . . a mystery to us," wrote Lt. Charles Keyes, 123rd Ohio Infantry. The 18th Connecticut's Cpl. Charles Lynch angrily recorded in his diary that night: "As seen by the men in the ranks, it was strange that a small force was ordered over that river to cope with Early's force, and the 6th Corps near by . . . some things are hard to understand in the life of a soldier."

The absence of support from the VI Corps proved particularly difficult to process among soldiers in Thoburn's command who believed that they stood on the verge of victory as a result of the strength of their position along the stone wall and the damaging impact of Union batteries in the bluffs. "We have . . . busied ourselves in speculating upon what we cannot help considering the blunder, by which, instead of the 6th corps crossing to support us, we were ordered to abandon a field, we had already won. We wonder who will crave the honor of giving that order," pondered a veteran of the 34th Massachusetts Infantry.

For decades after the conflict Thoburn's veterans, in the pages of the *National Tribune* (a weekly newspaper for Union veterans) and regimental histories, contended that with the aid of additional troops on the Shenandoah's western shore the battle would have ended differently. Twenty-eight years after the battle Pvt. Tilghman Lester, a veteran of the 54th Pennsylvania Infantry, argued in the *National Tribune*, "had the Sixth Corps come to the relief of the Eighth . . . the fight would have proven a victory for the Federals." William Edmonds, a veteran of the 4th West Virginia Infantry whose left arm was shattered by a Confederate bullet at Cool Spring, thought similarly. "There was a grand mistake made in not sending all the troops—that is, the Sixth and Nineteenth Corps— across the Shenandoah River to help us," Edmonds explained in the *National Tribune*.

Thoburn's troops were not the only ones baffled as to why Ricketts's division did not cross to the Shenandoah's western side. It too mystified some veterans of the VI Corps. The day after the battle Daniel Holt, a surgeon in the 121st New York, complained to his wife: "No certainty attends our movements. So far it appears to be the policy to let the rebels off without fighting them; whether from actual inability to cope with them and overcome them, or whether we love them too well as McClellan did at Antietam, I do not know." When some of Ricketts's veterans encountered Thoburn's troops on the grounds of the Retreat on the night of the 18th they expressed their disbelief that Wright and Ricketts refused to let them cross. "As we passed through the ranks of the 6th corps, after falling back," recalled Lt. Col. Thomas Wildes, Ricketts's "men frequently said to us 'We wanted to go over and help you but they wouldn't let us.'"

Some of Thoburn's veterans directed their anger at Maj. Gen. Wright. Corporal Charles Lynch confided to his diary that he and his comrades were "discouraged and mad, saying hard things about General Wright, Commander of the 6th Corps." Rumors circulated among Thoburn's troops that night that Wright intentionally withheld Ricketts's division to diminish Crook's reputation. "Rumor said that it was a plan of Gen. Wright, of the Sixth Corps, who ranked Gen. Crook, to disgrace the latter," recalled William Walker, chaplain of the 18th Connecticut. Walker did not want to believe that scenario but did not think it impossible. "It would be hard to believe this if similar meanness had not been exhibited before by other officers under more trying circumstances."

Not all of Thoburn's command possessed such far-fetched ideas. Lieutenant Colonel Wildes surmised that Wright's refusal to permit Ricketts to cross the river "can only be explained on the hypothesis, that it was not thought desirable to bring on a general engagement at that place, and at that time." An officer in the 123rd Ohio concluded that Wright "determined . . . that it would not be prudent to cross over more troops" because Thoburn's command found "the enemy in force."

While Thoburn's dejected troops, "wet . . . and generally covered with mud, from climbing the clay river banks," sought accountability on the Shenandoah's eastern bank, wounded Union soldiers who could not be evacuated from the river's western side focused on survival and avoiding capture. As "the last echo of the thundering cannon had died away," Lt. Leonidas Polk, 43rd North Carolina, recalled that the sounds of battle had been replaced by the "death-like silence save the groans of the wounded and dying and the soft murmuring of the blood-tinted waters of the Shenandoah whispering their funeral dirge." While stretcher bearers "moved to and fro on their mission of mercy like specters in that dread scene of death," Polk attempted to locate one wounded soldier—Lt. Col. Edward Murray, 5th New York Heavy Artillery. At some point prior to the battle's end Polk claimed to have discovered Murray, offered the New Yorker a drink from his canteen, and promised that if he "survived the battle . . . would give him [Murray] prompt attention." Amid the glow of the "pale yellow moon," Polk, along with the 43rd North Carolina's Capt. Cary Whitaker, discovered Murray and captured him. Polk ordered four litter bearers to carry Murray to a field hospital so doctors could assess the severity of his wounds—one to his right wrist and the other "to his back and over the region of the kidneys."

A native of Anson, North Carolina, Lt. Leonidas Polk began his Confederate service as a private in the 26th North Carolina on May 10, 1862. On February 2, 1863, Polk received a commission as a lieutenant in the 43rd North Carolina. After the conflict, Polk founded Polkton, North Carolina, and became the state's first commissioner of agriculture. Polk died in 1892. (wcnc)

Before Murray was carried away, Polk and Murray exchanged information. Both, as Polk recalled after the conflict, "made a mutual promise that if either survived the war, we would communicate with the other's family." Once Confederate surgeons treated Murray's wounds Murray believed, although not delighted at the prospect of being sent to a Confederate prison, he would not have survived without Polk's help. As the sun rose on July 19 Polk received a gift from Murray, his sword belt. "My dear friend, Lt. Polk," Murray wrote to Polk, "I send you my belt, as a slight token of my appreciation of your brotherly kindness to me. Send it to your children and tell them how you got it."

As Murray's belt made its way to Polk, Murray began his journey to Libby Prison in Richmond, Virginia. He spent the next eight months at Libby where, evidence indicates, "his wounds were treated by a surgeon of the Confederate army." After Murray was exchanged in March 1865 a Union surgeon at Camp Parole Hospital in Annapolis, Maryland, examined Murray and declared that he "was suffering much" from both wounds "particularly from the one in the back."

Murray's wounds plagued him for the rest of his life and ultimately contributed to his death on November 13, 1876. In the eleven years after the conflict's end, while Murray dealt with excessive pain "in the region of the kidneys" and frequent bouts of "hemorrhagic diarrhea"—all effects of the wound he suffered to his back at the battle of Cool Spring—Polk attempted to make contact with him. "Some months after the war closed I began to write to officials and other prominent gentlemen in New York State to ascertain the fate of Col. Murray," Polk explained to a reporter for the *National Tribune*. After those initial efforts failed, Polk, who became an important figure in North Carolina politics after the conflict, including the state's first commissioner of agriculture, stopped trying.

However, when Polk began publishing a weekly newspaper in the mid-1870s, the *Ansonian*, and penned a series of articles about his military service, his curiosity about Murray's fate was reinvigorated when Polk started writing about his service in the Shenandoah Valley. "Reviewing these old war scenes intensified my desire and purpose to ascertain the fate of Col. Murray," Polk recalled. Polk penned another letter, this time directly to Murray in New York City; however, Polk never received a reply. Undaunted in his quest, Polk sent his sketch of the battle, as he remembered, "to a number of papers in New York State" in the autumn of 1876. Several weeks later, one New York editor sent Polk a note with the sad news that Murray had passed away. Approximately one month after Murray's death, his widow, Mary, wrote Polk. She explained that her husband did not receive Polk's letter until "about a year" after Polk sent it. Mary Murray wrote to Polk that her husband wanted to respond but could not in his weakened state. "My letter did not reach him until about a year after it was written, and after he was confined to his bed," Polk noted. Although Murray wrote no response, Murray's widow claimed that Polk's "letter gave him great joy and inspired a hope for his final recovery; that he loved to dwell upon it, and talked about the event, but that he never regained sufficient strength to answer it." After learning of Murray's death, Polk offered to return the belt to Mrs. Murray. "This she declined," Polk explained to a correspondent for the *National Tribune*, "with tenderest expressions of magnanimity and generous thanks for my kindness to her husband, and stating that she knew she could best carry out his wishes by allowing me to keep the belt."

From the time of Murray's death until Polk's on June 11, 1892, Polk maintained a relationship with Murray's family. He visited New York City in 1885 and spent "some days" with them and exchanged "occasional letters." One of the last letters Polk received from Murray's family came in the spring of 1892. In it the family requested "that for the associations connected with it" Polk return the belt. Polk "readily agreed" to the request and "cheerfully surrender[ed] the belt."

As Confederate litter bearers carried Murray to a field hospital that night, Capt. Whitaker ventured there too. Not to check on Murray, but to discover the fate of his friend and cousin 2nd Lt. William Beavans. "Smiling Billy," as Beavans was known prior to the war by admirers in Halifax County, North Carolina, and Whitaker served together since the war's outset, first in the 1st North Carolina and then in the 43rd North Carolina. Amid the heart-rending scene of the field hospital for Rodes's division, Whitaker located Beavans. Struck by a bullet in the right leg below the knee prior to Rodes's final assault, Beavans was in excruciating pain. Surgeons in Rodes's division, like their Union counterparts, managed as best they could to care for the approximately 300 Confederates wounded during the fighting, but it would not be until the following morning that a surgeon examined Beavans and deemed amputation necessary.

Somewhat remarkably Beavans recorded a few thoughts about his wound, suffering, and amputation in his diary. The pain Beavans felt is evident through his handwriting. An examination of his diary reveals neat penmanship prior to suffering his wound. After he received his wound, his handwriting became

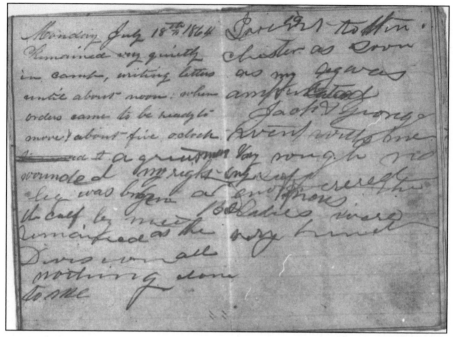

This page from the diary of 2nd Lt. William Beavans reveals the excruciating pain Beavans endured after being wounded at Cool Spring. (unc)

nearly indecipherable—a powerful visible reminder of the excruciating pain he endured. "Grievously wounded my right leg was broken at the calf by [a] mus[ket] ball. Remained at the Division [hospital] all [night] nothing done to me," Beavans wrote. After his amputation the following morning Beavans's wrote of his ordeal: "my leg was amputated . . . very rough no drug suffered enormous."

Late that night, while Beavans waited for a surgeon to amputate his leg, Cary Whitaker reflected on the ordeal which his twenty-four-year-old comrade confronted. Although saddened, as Whitaker recorded in his diary, "very sorry to hear this . . . so hard for a gay fine looking man in the bloom of his youth, to be mutilated in this way," Whitaker believed there a silver lining to Beavans's loss of his right leg below the knee—Beavans could return home to civilian life. "One consolation is that it might have been worse, that he is now out of the war, the loss of a leg may be the saving of his life," Whitaker confessed in his diary. Five days after the battle another of Beavans's comrades, 2nd Lt. George Whitaker Wills, expressed similar thoughts. Wills, who was killed two months later at the Third Battle of Winchester, wrote that Beavans "will be clear of the war; and that is a consideration,

since men's lives are not now insured from one day to another, and he tho[ugh] with one leg, is probably better off than any of us with two."

Beavans, however, would not be "better off." After amputation at the field hospital he was transported to the York Hospital in Winchester. As Beavans lay in a bed in the building on South Market Street (present-day South Cameron Street), which once served as the Valley Female Institute, his condition worsened as he contracted typhoid fever. On July 31, in his final hours, Beavans informed Kate Shepherd, a local civilian who had been caring for him, that he would love "to get well for the sake of my parents." At 5:00 p.m. that day Beavans died. Initially buried in the Shepherd family plot, Beavans's body was later reinterred in the Stonewall Confederate Cemetery in Winchester.

While surgeons on both sides of the Shenandoah tended to the wounded that night, burial parties began their grisly task. The battle of Cool Spring ultimately claimed 140 lives (75 Union and 65 Confederate); however, records indicate that 82 dead soldiers lay on the western side of the Shenandoah River that night (47 Union and 35 Confederate).

Site of the York Hospital in Winchester where William Beavans died on July 31, 1864. (jn)

Colonel James Wood, a native of Rowan County, North Carolina, received his commission as colonel of the 4th North Carolina Infantry on May 19, 1864. Two months later he was killed at Cool Spring. A fellow North Carolinian wrote that Wood was "a young man of much promise, and a model soldier; brave, gallant, and faithful." Wood's body was removed from the battlefield and sent home for burial in the Third Creek Presbyterian Church Cemetery in Rowan County. (wcnc)

While the battle's death toll increased in the ensuing days as those mortally wounded succumbed to their wounds, some of the Union dead had been taken across the Shenandoah River by comrades, among them Pvt. James Haverfield, 170th Ohio Infantry. "Shot and killed instantly," Haverfield's cousin, Sgt. James Haverfield, "aided by a comrade, carried him to the rear and across the river, and there they laid him to rest in a small garden." Somewhat similarly, not all Confederates killed during the fighting on the 18th were buried on the battlefield. The remains of Col. James Wood, 4th North Carolina, were taken from the field and sent home for burial in the Third Creek Presbyterian Church in Rowan County, North Carolina.

As Capt. Robert Park, 12th Alabama, who oversaw a burial party, walked the field that night, he encountered the body of a North Carolinian. Although Park could not remember the soldier's identity he recalled that on numerous occasions throughout the conflict that he, and others in Rodes's division, repeatedly urged the soldier to not wear his "silk ('stove pipe') hat" into battle because it made him "conspicuous." When Park encountered the slain Tarheel, one of twenty North Carolinians killed, Park "was pained to see the well-known tall hat, and upon nearing it, to recognize the handsome, good-natured face and manly form of the gallant wearer lying cold in death. He had been shot in the head."

While burial details carried out their somber duty other contingents of Confederates took what they could from the Union dead. For example, Lt. Col. J. Floyd King encouraged soldiers, such as artillerist Milton Humphreys who needed a new pair of shoes, to take what they needed from the dead. "My shoes were very bad," Humphreys wrote in his diary. "I went to Col. King and asked him if I could not be supplied. We were in a field full of dead briers & the soles were virtually off my shoes. He told me to 'go down in front and pull a pair off a dead Yankee,'" Humphreys recalled. While Humphreys ultimately decided to not do this for fear that "a sharpshooter might pick" him "off" evidence indicates that "many" of the Union dead had been completely "stripped." While Confederate chaplain James Sheeran mentioned nothing in his diary about Confederate soldiers taking clothing items, he noted that night that "we collected an immense number of small arms after this battle" from the Union dead.

As both sides took stock of the day's fighting, cared for the wounded, and buried the dead, uncertainty loomed about whether or not the fighting would resume in the morning. "We slept in line of battle, on our arms, ready for action, near the battlefield," recorded Capt. Park in his diary. That night along the Union picket line along the Shenandoah's eastern bank, Capt. Elisha Hunt Rhodes noted that he "could hear the Rebels talking and speculating upon the chances of being driven back by the Yankees at daylight." All speculation would soon end as the new day's sun rose from behind the Blue Ridge on the morning of July 19.

Captain Elisha Hunt Rhodes, 2nd Rhode Island Infantry, was among those who picketed the Shenandoah River on the night of July 18 and the early hours of the following day. Rhodes enlisted in the 2nd Rhode Island as a corporal on June 5, 1861. By the war's end, he rose to the rank of colonel. After the conflict, Rhodes was active in the Grand Army of the Republic and served as the vice president of the Sheridan's Veterans' Association, which visited the Shenandoah Valley in 1883 and 1885. Rhodes died in 1917. (loc)

"Never to Be Forgotten"

CHAPTER SEVEN
JULY 19–20, 1864

As the sun's first rays shone over the battlefield on the morning of July 19, the 2nd Rhode Island's Capt. Elisha Hunt Rhodes—part of the Union force that picketed the Shenandoah River's eastern bank—spied four of Thoburn's veterans, wounded the previous day, attempting to reach the safety of the river's eastern shore. Once in the river, Rhodes heard a "Rebel officer" command Confederate pickets "to fire upon them." Customarily, Rhodes made it a practice when on picket to avoid shooting, "as it is murderous business," but this time he broke convention and returned fire. Rhodes explained in his diary: "when I heard this officer order his men to shoot wounded men I ordered my line to open fire which they did with much spirit." When the Union picket line opened with their Spencer rifles a veteran of the 37th Massachusetts recalled that "the Confederates found themselves at such a disadvantage when opposed to the Spencer that they called out asking what kind of a 'shooting iron' it was." Captain Rhodes recalled that the Union pickets did not respond verbally, but instead replied with "another volley."

After the battle ended, a Confederate soldier from North Carolina noted that the Shenandoah River, pictured here looking north, had "been so reddened with human gore." (jn)

While no significant fighting took place on July 19, the air oftentimes reverberated with the sounds of the "lively interchange of shots by the picket lines" and occasional fire from a Union cannon in the bluffs that attempted to disrupt activities of Confederate batteries in the area. For instance, Confederate artillerist Milton Humphreys explained in his diary that day that each time he and his comrades in Chapman's Battery attempted to water the horses at "a very large spring a few hundred yards away in rear of our position," a Union cannon "would throw a shell among them." Although the fire from Union cannon did not do "any damage" the spectacle unnerved Gen. Early. As Early watched shells land near the horses he shouted 'Scatter out!' and directed the artillerists to 'take these horses away' as he feared, and rightfully so, that 'they are going to be shot!'"

As picket and sporadic cannon fire continued throughout what the chaplain of the 18th Connecticut characterized as "an extremely hot day," Union troops spied a flurry of Confederate activity on the Shenandoah's western side, the most significant of which was evacuating the wounded to hospitals in Winchester. Throughout the day Confederate ambulances carried the lion's share of the approximately 300 Confederate soldiers wounded during the battle to the various makeshift hospitals in the community. Mary Greenhow Lee, one of Winchester's staunchest Confederates, recorded in her diary that day: "Long trains of ambulances came in bringing the wounded from the fight of yesterday. . . . The ambulances have been coming all day." When Lee, who regularly aided the wounded at the York Hospital located several blocks from her home on Market Street (present-day Cameron Street), saw the steady stream of wounded she went to her kitchen and "made a large supply of panada & carried it up & down the line of ambulances." The day's excessive heat made the task, as Lee remembered, quite "fatiguing."

Among the Confederates brought to one of the hospitals in Winchester was Sgt. Aaron Leonidas DeArmond, 30th North Carolina. By the time of the battle of Cool Spring the thirty-seven-year-old farmer from Mecklenburg County, North Carolina, had his share of unfortunate experiences on the battlefield. In addition to being captured twice, at Antietam on September 17, 1862, and Kelly's Ford on November 7, 1863, DeArmond suffered a wound to his left arm at Fredericksburg. Although only thirty-seven by the time of the clash at Cool Spring, DeArmond's horrific wartime experiences aged him well beyond his years. "I am getting grey very fast, my beard is nearly white. . . . I expect my head will be right white before this war is ended," DeArmond wrote his wife Nancy. A piece of shrapnel, according to one chronicler, "mutilated" DeArmond during the battle of Cool Spring. After doctors treated him in Winchester he was sent to Confederate General Hospital in Charlottesville, Virginia. He arrived in Charlottesville on July 25. Six days later he was transferred to General Hospital No. 9 in Richmond. Remarkably, DeArmond recovered enough from his wound to be granted a furlough to convalesce at home. Unfortunately, his condition worsened as he neared his farm in Mecklenburg County. On August 19, less than three miles from his home, DeArmond became so overcome with exhaustion that he sought a place to rest. The nearest shelter he found was a chicken coop. He went inside, laid down, and died. DeArmond left behind a wife and four children. He was buried in Sardis Presbyterian Church Cemetery in Charlotte, North Carolina.

While some Confederates evacuated wounded from the battlefield, others in Early's army made preparations to prevent Union forces from attempting another crossing of the Shenandoah River. Along the river's western edge Union forces spied Confederates constructing defenses. A veteran of the 34th Massachusetts recalled: "We can easily see the Rebels now at work. . . . [They] seem to be building barricades along the river bank."

Despite the precautionary measures Early's Confederates took to protect against a potential Union assault and sporadic firing throughout the day, a survey of letters and diaries from Early's troops reveal that few, if any, believed that Wright would renew the fight. "The campaign is virtually ended," Confederate general Gabriel Wharton wrote to his wife, Nannie, on July 19. "Genl Crook came over the River yesterday evening, but we whipped him back. . . . Don't think

Brigadier General William Averell, a native of New York, graduated from West Point in 1855. Although a competent cavalry commander, Union general Philip Sheridan, who detested Averell, removed him from command in late September 1864. After the conflict, in addition to serving as U.S. consul general to British North America, Averell received several patents for various inventions, perhaps most notably one in 1878 for his "Improvement in Asphaltic Pavement." Averell died in 1900. (loc)

Genl. Crook will try us again," Wharton explained. The 5th Alabama's Joel Calvin McDiarmid concurred and believed, as he confided to his diary, "The Yanks were satisfied with their thrashing."

Although Early's veterans appeared confident that the command which pursued them from Washington posed no threat, Early learned of another potential hazard to his army that day—that a Union force commanded by Brig. Gen. William Averell "was moving from Martinsburg to Winchester." If Early remained in his position he risked being sandwiched between two Union forces. "As the position I held near Berryville left my trains exposed to expeditions in the rear from Martinsburg and Harper's Ferry, I determined to concentrate my forces near Strasburg, so as to enable me to put the trains in safety and then move out and attack the enemy," Early explained.

Late that night Early issued orders for his command to head west toward Winchester and then south toward Strasburg. As Early's directive trickled down to his regiments some grumbled as they still sought some much-needed rest. "About 11 p.m. we received marching orders. This was too bad; we were just enjoying in anticipation a good night's rest," explained a Confederate chaplain from Louisiana. Artillerist Milton Humphreys echoed: "At night we lay down, but shortly afterwards were quietly stirred up, and amused to the reality that another night march was before us. No one who has never tried it can know how much one suffers from sleeplessness on these night marches, after being fatigued."

On the morning of the 20th, Wright ordered Montague, who commanded the Union picket line since the battle ended on the night of the 18th, to cross to the Shenandoah's western side. Fully expecting Confederate pickets to contest the crossing, Montague carefully positioned a contingent of troops on Parker's Island to provide support to the remaining troops from the 37th Massachusetts and 2nd Rhode Island who would cross to the Shenandoah's western shore. The 37th's Capt. Joshua Loomis reportedly "set foot on the coveted shore first." Once they reached the position which shielded Thoburn's command on the 18th, Montague ordered the troops to press forward. One Massachusetts soldier recalled that as they moved out of the road, over the stone wall, and up the slopes toward the Cool Spring mansion they fully expected "the flash of hostile rifles in their faces." Fortunately for Montague's detachment, Early's Confederates were gone. "It was a bloodless victory . . . but none the less it was to those engaged a thrilling episode," recalled one of the 37th's veterans.

Once Wright received word that Early's army had withdrawn westward he directed his command, around noon, to cross the Shenandoah. As Union troops entered the river a thunderstorm, characterized by the 121st New York's Surgeon Daniel Holt as "a real ripper," drenched Wright's command. First Lieutenant Charles Keyes, 123rd Ohio, thought "it quite laughable to see some of the men attempt to keep dry" as they waded the river. Any jocularity displayed during the crossing, however, ended abruptly when they reached the other side and gazed upon the horrifying scene of how Early's Confederates treated the Union dead. In many instances the dead, according to assistant surgeon Alexander Neil, 12th West Virginia, "were only half buried, heads & feet sticking out of the ground." William Walker, the chaplain of the 18th Connecticut, thought the practice, one he had witnessed before, unconscionable. "Found that the rebels, as usual, had outraged the dead, leaving them but half buried. . . . It was a painful, sickening sight. It made one feel indignant and even revengeful toward the inhuman creatures who could be guilty of such acts of wicked barbarity . . . Everlasting infamy will be attached to the memory of the rebel leaders who allowed the soldiery to treat with so much neglect and cruelty their patriotic opponents in war," Walker wrote.

While the disturbing scene unnerved Union troops, it was far from unique. In a battle's aftermath, as historian Drew Gilpin Faust argued in her groundbreaking study of death during the Civil War, soldiers from a victorious army charged with burying the dead of both sides "predictably gave precedence to their own casualties" and buried them with greater care. Additionally, as Faust posits, the "half buried" condition of the Union dead potentially stemmed from the Confederates' desire to conceal their own losses and highlight those of their counterparts. Also, the lack of care given by Confederates to burying

Surgeon Daniel Holt, a native of New York, graduated from medical school in Cincinnati, Ohio, in 1853. He was commissioned assistant surgeon of the 121st New York on August 27, 1862. Holt contracted tuberculosis during his military service. It forced Holt to resign his commission in the autumn of 1864. Holt died in 1868. (ahec)

the Union dead could simply be the product of insufficient time. Regardless of why Confederates buried Thoburn's dead in the way they did, the visceral reaction to it by Union veterans on July 20 is one that soldiers on both sides experienced throughout the war when confronted with the gruesome sight. "Burials like these dehumanized the dead and appalled many of the living," Faust concluded.

In addition to the ghastly scene of the "half buried" Union dead, some troops in Wright's command reported that Confederates had stripped "many" completely "naked . . . every stitch of clothing having been taken." While justifiably perceived as disrespectful, a broader perspective about how troops pilfered from the dead in a battle's aftermath reveals that what Confederates did to the Union dead after Cool Spring was not unusual. Faust's study reveals that soldiers "desperate for clothing" took things "frequently" from the dead usually "with little feeling of propriety or remorse." Although no evidence exists to support this occurred at Cool Spring, Faust convincingly demonstrates that the living at times even took things from the dead of their own army.

As 2nd Lt. William Byron Henry, 116th Ohio, walked the battlefield that afternoon he discovered the body of Pvt. Samuel Hayes "stripped by the fiends and left unburied." Henry, who had seen much death and destruction since mustering into the regiment as a first sergeant on August 12, 1862, possessed a special affinity for Hayes. Two weeks after the battle he explained to his sister that the Confederates "robbed my little dead boy." For Henry this was no longer war, it was personal. Henry admitted to his sister that the manner in which Confederates treated the body of the nineteen-year-old Hayes motivated him "to retaliate upon the carcasses of live rebels." While Henry's reaction is understandable, it is not exceptional among either Union or Confederate soldiers. The death of cherished comrades, according to historian Jonathan Steplyk, "provoked" soldiers throughout the conflict "to exact lethal revenge."

As Union troops moved over the battlefield that afternoon they also discovered that some of the Union wounded who remained on the field had been victimized by Confederates who "robbed

them of everything, even their hats, boots, & coats."
Precisely how many wounded remained on the
field on July 20 is unclear. Surgeon Alexander Neil
estimated approximately "three hundred" made it
to the Shenandoah's eastern side by July 19. With
only 301 Union soldiers reported wounded during
the engagement, Neil's estimate is more than likely
somewhat exaggerated.

Nonetheless, wounded Union soldiers who had
not been "carried . . . off to different localities,"
remained on the battlefield until the 20th. Among
them were two veterans of the 54th Pennsylvania,
Privates John Hensel and Joseph Atchison. Hensel,
who enlisted in the regiment on October 1, 1861,
received two wounds during the battle. The first was
to his left hand. A second Confederate bullet struck
Hensel in his "left leg just below the knee cap" during
the regiment's withdrawal. Atchison received an
undisclosed wound during the regiment's withdrawal.
The two residents of Somerset County, Pennsylvania,
as Atchison recalled, were "wounded at about the
same time, and we both lay on the field . . . not a great
distance from each other and remained in the hands
of the Rebels" until Union forces "recaptured" them
on July 20. Both survived their wounds. Hensel died
on June 30, 1898, from apoplexy. Atchison, one of the
last surviving Union veterans in Berlin, Pennsylvania,
died on April 17, 1929. A reporter from Meyersdale,
Pennsylvania, lamented: "The death of Joseph
Atchison . . . reduced Berlin's thinning ranks of the
Grand Army of the Republic to four."

As surgeons tended to the wounded, loaded them
into ambulances, and sent them to Harpers Ferry for
additional treatment, portions of Wright's command,
tired of the "hard living," as the 121st New York's
Daniel Holt recorded in his diary, of "hard tack and
pork" foraged for food. Troops in the 11th Vermont
Infantry commandeered beehives, soldiers from the
2nd Rhode Island took chickens, and troops from the
9th New York Heavy Artillery seized "sheep, hogs,
and bacon." Veterans from the 18th Connecticut
enlisted the aid of an unidentified Black male to assist
in their search of something more sumptuous than the
soldier's traditional fare. The "negro acted as a guide
to the several places where produce of all sorts was

stored away to elude the vigilance of the men," one of the regiment's veterans recalled. Additionally, the Black guide directed the Connecticut troops to "a farm house not far away" from the battlefield where several men from the regiment wounded during the battle had been hiding. Among those discovered was Pvt. Richmond Corey. A native of Lebanon, Connecticut, Corey, who served earlier in the conflict in the 3rd Connecticut Infantry, mustered into Company C, 18th Connecticut on March 6, 1864. When Corey set eyes on his comrades on July 20, the thirty-four-year old—"badly wounded" in the left leg—seemed, in the estimation of the regiment's chaplain, "glad enough to be in Union lines once more." Damage to Corey's left leg was so severe that surgeons had no other recourse but amputation. For the remainder of his life Corey's debility prevented him from working. Awarded a $30 per month pension from the United States government, Corey spent most of his remaining life residing in homes for disabled volunteer soldiers. Records indicate that he entered the National Home for Disabled Volunteer Soldiers in Togus, Maine, in 1869. By 1880 Corey transferred to the National Home for Disabled Volunteer Soldiers in Hampton, Virginia. Corey died there on July 18, 1887, the battle of Cool Spring's twenty-third anniversary. He is buried in Hampton National Cemetery, grave 5896.

Although the foraging expedition yielded an array of foodstuffs and led to the rescue of wounded comrades, the day did not come without its perils. George Carpenter, a veteran of the 8th Vermont Infantry, recalled that during "a terrific thunderstorm that afternoon," one which Carpenter believed produced a "tornado," an unidentified soldier "belonging to a New York regiment was killed by the lightning." As Lt. William Byron Henry was composing a letter to his sister about the tragic fate of Samuel Hayes, the report of a musket shot startled him. Henry interrupted his thoughts about Hayes' death and wrote: "Bang goes a musket followed by a groan some poor fellow has shot himself." Henry later learned that it was accidental; a soldier in the 1st West Virginia Cavalry "shot off three of his fingers." Somewhat nonchalantly, Henry explained to his sister that "such things are frequent in the Army."

While portions of Wright's command foraged and aided the wounded, another portion of Wright's force marched west toward Berryville to determine Early's precise whereabouts. The force proceeded west for approximately four miles but could not locate Early. "We moved very cautiously, with skirmishers, two or three miles in the direction of Berryville, without finding the enemy," recalled a veteran of the 15th New Jersey Infantry. A Vermont officer wrote similarly, "We went out three or four miles and found no enemy." Early's absence from the immediate area convinced Wright that Early was departing the Shenandoah Valley for Lee's army at Petersburg and no longer presented a threat to invade the North or threaten Washington. One officer in Wright's force concluded simply: "Early had apparently returned in haste to Richmond." That night, satisfied that "Early had retreated southward," Wright believed his pursuit of Early complete and that he could return the VI and XIX Corps "to Washington and thence to Petersburg without delay." Wright explained simply to Grant that he conceived "the object of the expedition to be accomplished."

Despite the belief, as one Union officer recalled, that "all the General Officers coincided in the opinion that the object of the expedition was accomplished" and Early no longer posed a threat in the Shenandoah

One wonders what might have been the fate of Early's army had Wright pushed his command further west. Today, little remains of the Rutherford's Farm battlefield. This photo, taken by the author in the late 1990s, shows that portion of the battlefield situated on the west side of the Martinsburg Pike north of Winchester. Today, this area is the site of a shopping center. (jn)

Valley, Vermonter Aldace Walker did not seem so certain. "The conclusion that Early had abandoned the Valley seems to have been hastily reached, and perhaps was founded rather on what he was expected to do, than on actual information obtained concerning his movements," Walker wrote. Walker's assessment proved accurate. Early did not leave the Valley, nor did he ever have any intention of doing so in late July. Had Wright pushed ten miles further west beyond Berryville to Winchester, he would have discovered approximately 5,000 Confederates under command of Maj. Gen. Stephen Dodson Ramseur. Early kept Ramseur in Winchester to "cover that place . . . while the sick and wounded were being removed, and the other divisions" of his army marched toward Strasburg. Additionally, Wright could have lent critical support to Brig. Gen. William Averell whose force, approximately half the size of Ramseur's, engaged and remarkably defeated Ramseur's command on Winchester's northern outskirts at the battle of Rutherford's Farm on July 20. While engaging in what-if scenarios can sometimes be a fruitless endeavor for a historian, it is not unreasonable to surmise that had Averell's approximately 2,700 troops had additional support, Ramseur could have been driven from Winchester, the pursuit of Early's army continued, and additional punishment inflicted on Early's command.

Averell's victory at the battle of Rutherford's Farm, coupled with Early's decisive victory over General Crook's command at the Second Battle of Kernstown on July 24, and the potential opportunities Wright might have missed by ordering the VI and XIX Corps from the Valley on July 20, prompted some Northern journalists to speculate about what might have been. A correspondent for the *New York World* believed that had Wright continued "the pursuit ten hours longer" on July 20 the Union forces in the Shenandoah Valley could potentially "have defeated Early." The correspondent freely admitted that such a pursuit came with risk and recognized that Wright could also "have been himself defeated." Other newspapers throughout the North echoed this criticism.

Some officials in the War Department thought Wright erred in withdrawing the bulk of the pursuit force from the Shenandoah Valley, among them

Assistant Secretary of War Charles Dana. "The pursuit of Early proved, on the whole, an egregious blunder . . . Wright . . . drew back as soon as he got where he might have done something worth while. As it was, Early escaped." While troops in Wright's force might not have viewed the situation so pessimistically, they recognized that the departure of the VI and XIX Corps marked the end of Wright's pursuit. John Mead Gould, the adjutant of the 29th Maine, wrote in his diary on July 20: "So this raiding campaign has ended. The rebels have certainly done well in it accomplishing all that they could expect and getting off unhurt." Gould, however, waited to pass final judgment on whether or not Early's victory at Cool Spring and the departure of the VI and XIX Corps would yield any significantly positive results for the Confederate war effort. "How much they have effected toward putting the Confederacy upon a firmer basis remains to be seen," Gould wrote. A correspondent for the *New York Herald* concurred. "We must await further news . . . before it is quite possible to say whether we ought not to rejoice over this last invasion."

The 29th Maine's John Mead Gould waited to pass judgment about the impact of Wright's pursuit. (np)

In retrospect Wright's decision to not push further west toward Winchester proved ill-advised, and his decision to move the VI and XIX Corps to Washington and then Petersburg appeared premature. However, it is imperative to underscore that Wright felt pressure from Grant to return those forces as soon as possible. While Grant never desired to put Washington in harm's way, explaining to Halleck on July 21 that Halleck could "retain Wright's Command until the departure of Early is assured," Grant did not want the VI and XIX Corps to remain any longer than necessary. "I want if possible to get the 6th & 19th Corps here [Petersburg]," Grant explained. When Wright sent one of his staff officers to Washington ahead of the return of the two corps, Wright sent a note to Halleck which reiterated that his decision to quit the Valley once the threat from Early disappeared was influenced by Grant's instructions over the previous week. On the night of July 22 Halleck telegraphed Grant: "A staff officer of Genl Wright arrived last night with a dispatch dated 1:30 p.m. of the 21st. Acting on your previous orders he had given up the pursuit & would reach Washington today."

Twelve days after the battle of Cool Spring, Confederate Brig. Gen. John McCausland brought fiery destruction to Chambersburg, Pennsylvania. (loc)

Early's defeat of Crook at Kernstown on July 24 was followed by additional furor when Confederate cavalry commanded by Brig. Gen. John McCausland's burned Chambersburg, Pennsylvania, at the end of July. All of this prompted the forces Wright returned to the nation's capital to be sent back to the Valley less than one week later to, as a Vermont veteran explained, "follow him [Early] closely, and keep the hostile army at bay as far as possible." Wright's pursuit appeared a failure. Assistant Secretary of War Charles Dana bluntly declared that Wright's pursuit "accomplished nothing."

While what happened along the banks of the Shenandoah River in Clarke County might have meant nothing strategically significant to the Union war effort in Virginia, to Thoburn's veterans it meant a great deal. Although tactically defeated, the doggedness they displayed against unfavorable odds became a source of pride for them in the battle's immediate aftermath and for decades after the conflict, as they claimed that the battle's fortunes could have been different had Ricketts's regiments supported them as originally directed. For the Union soldiers wounded and the families of those killed, including troops from the VI Corps not engaged in the battle but struck by errant Confederate artillery shells, the battle of Cool Spring proved the war's most significant moment.

To Confederates engaged at Cool Spring, the battle's importance exceeded its status as another victory in the Shenandoah Valley. For those wounded in the fight and those, such as the 4th North Carolina's John Alexander Stikeleather, who lost two great friends during the battle, Cool Spring meant a great deal. Years after the conflict, as Stikeleather reflected on the fight and the fate of comrades Privates Martin Snow and David Bustle, both of whom served with Stikeleather in the regiment's color guard and died on the battlefield, he did not use the battle's size, strategic significance, or tactical results as litmus tests to measure Cool Spring's importance in the Civil War's broader context. The loss of people he "loved . . . like a brother" made the battle along the banks of the Shenandoah one of the conflict's most significant to him.

For those engaged at Cool Spring, whether Union or Confederate, the battle derived its significance not from its outcome, but from its multifarious impacts on soldiers and their families. Those personal consequences, coupled with the engagement's intense combat, branded Cool Spring, at least in the estimation of Confederate veteran John Alexander Stikeleather, as a battle that deserved "never to be forgotten."

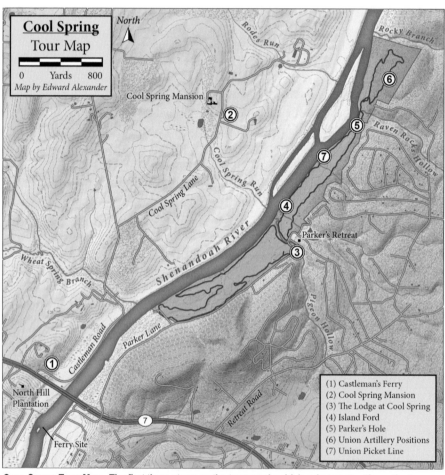

Cool Spring Tour Map

0　Yards　800

Map by Edward Alexander

North

Cool Spring Mansion ② ①

⑥

⑤

Raven Rocks Hollow

Rocky Branch

Rodes Run

Cool Spring Run

Cool Spring Lane

⑦

④

Parker's Retreat

③

Shenandoah River

Pigeon Hollow

Wheat Spring Branch

Castleman Road

Parker Lane

① North Hill Plantation

⑦

Retreat Road

Ferry Site

(1) Castleman's Ferry
(2) Cool Spring Mansion
(3) The Lodge at Cool Spring
(4) Island Ford
(5) Parker's Hole
(6) Union Artillery Positions
(7) Union Picket Line

COOL SPRING TOUR MAP—The first three stops on the tour require driving, but at stop three, the tour follows a walking trail. Please use caution while driving on state roads.

Touring the Battle of Cool Spring
APPENDIX A

Fortunately, through the efforts of the American Battlefield Trust and Shenandoah University, much of the land upon which the battle of Cool Spring occurred is preserved. This tour guides users to sites where the fighting occurred on July 17 and 18. Additionally, it directs users to locations with important connections to the battle and its aftermath. Please make certain that you respect signs and regulations at the various sites included on this tour.

Stop 1 – Castleman's Ferry

Begin at the intersection of Route 7 and Shenandoah River—north side of Route 7 and east side of Shenandoah River).

GPS: 39.12582°N, 77.89368°W

This is where Lt. Gen. Jubal A. Early's Army of the Valley began crossing the Shenandoah River on July 16, 1864. On July 17, 1864, Confederates from Maj. Gen. John B. Gordon's division formed in the area you are now situated to prevent Union troops commanded by Brig. Gen. Alfred Duffié and Col. James Mulligan from crossing the Shenandoah River. Throughout the day on July 17 and the following morning, Union forces moved through Snickers Gap, located to your front, and launched repeated assaults against this position. All of these efforts proved futile.

Modern-day view of area near Castleman's Ferry from the Shenandoah River's western shore. (jn)

    ## TO STOP 2

From the parking area turn right onto Castleman Road. Follow Castleman Road for 1.1 miles and turn right onto Cool Spring Road (entrance to Holy Cross Abbey) and follow Cool Spring Road for 0.7 miles and turn right into the Holy Cross Abbey gift shop parking lot.

901 Cool Spring Lane, Berryville, VA 22611
GPS coordinates: 39.14477°N, 77.87635°W

Stop 2 – Holy Cross Abbey

Modern-day view of the Cool Spring mansion at Our Lady of the Holy Cross Abbey. (jn)

The site of Our Lady of the Holy Cross Abbey, a Roman Catholic Monastery of the Cistercian Order, following the rule of St. Benedict, these pastoral fields are where much of the clash on July 18, 1864, took place. If you park in the Holy Cross Abbey gift shop parking lot, stand along Cool Spring Road (the road upon which you entered) and look north to view the limestone Cool Spring mansion.

Once you view the Cool Spring mansion standing in the gift shop parking lot, orient yourself looking east toward the Shenandoah River. On this ground to your front on the afternoon of July 18, 1864, troops from Brig. Gen. Gabriel Wharton's division deployed. To the north of the gift shop is where Maj. Gen. Robert Rodes's division launched his flank assault. While the gift shop is open to the public at various times, please note that exploration of the fields is not permitted. Please be respectful of this site and the important and prayerful work being performed here by the monks of the Holy Cross Abbey.

TO STOP 3

From the parking area turn left onto Cool Spring Road and follow for 0.7 miles. Turn left onto Castleman Road and follow for 1.1 miles until you reach Route 7. Turn left onto Route 7 (get into left lane), follow for 0.4 miles and turn left onto Parker Lane (this will be the first left after you cross the bridge spanning the Shenandoah River). Follow Parker Lane for 1.3 miles and park in either the lot to your front or left.

1400 Parker Lane, Bluemont, VA 20135
GPS coordinates: 39.13528°N, 77.86897°W

Stop 3 – Shenandoah University's River Campus at Cool Spring Battlefield

LEFT: View of the Lodge at Shenandoah University's River Campus at Cool Spring Battlefield (jn)

BELOW: The kiosk at Shenandoah University's River Campus at Cool Spring Battlefield offers an array of information about the site's history. (jn)

This 195-acre property, acquired by the Civil War Trust (now American Battlefield Trust) and entrusted to Shenandoah University's stewardship in 2013, was once part of an approximately 1,100-acre plantation, the Retreat, owned by Judge Richard Parker, the jurist who presided over John Brown's trial in the autumn of 1859. The Lodge, the large log structure, is owned by Shenandoah University and contains an exhibition about the battle and its aftermath. The exhibition contains a number of artifacts related to the battle. The exhibition area is open as volunteer

staffing at the site permits. Trails at the site are open throughout the year from sunrise until sunset. Please note that the remaining four stops on this tour are exclusively on foot.

 TO STOP 4

Proceed west on foot from the lodge to the kiosk, located near the end of the parking lot. The kiosk contains additional information about the site. Once you have visited the kiosk take the paved path, located to your left, to Island Ford. As you proceed on the path you will catch a view of Judge Parker's Retreat to your right. Please note that the Retreat is privately owned. The distance on foot is 0.1 mile.

GPS coordinates: 39.13772°N, 77.87068°W

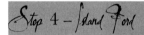

Around 3:30 p.m. on July 18, 1864, Col. George Wells's brigade led the van of Col. Joseph Thoburn's advance down Parker's Ford Road to this point. The road that runs to the left of Parker's Retreat, if you are looking at the home with the Shenandoah River to your back, is all that remains of Parker's Ford Road. Troops from Maj. Jesse Richardson's 42nd Virginia Infantry, positioned on the opposite shore, attempted to contest the crossing, but proved no match for Wells's brigade. Once Wells's command drove off the Virginians, Thoburn crossed his division here. Depending on the time of year the view from Island Ford can afford a view of the battlefield's contours not visible from Holy Cross Abbey. Colonel Thoburn positioned his command in two main lines, one approximately seventy-yards from the river's edge and the other along the river's west bank. A skirmish line deployed beyond Thoburn's line was situated seventy-five yards beyond the river's edge. During the time of year when trees are devoid of foliage one can see the ground sloping upward from the river's edge. The crest that is visible marks the location of Thoburn's first line.

 TO STOP 5

Continue on the paved path, keeping the Shenandoah River on your left side, for 0.78 miles. You will see a rise of high ground to your left front and a bench. This vantage point will provide you a view of Parker's Hole.

GPS coordinates: 39.14601°N, 77.86264°W

Stop 5 – Parker's Hole

The greenish-tinted rushing water in front of you is Parker's Hole. While much of the Shenandoah River was fordable in the summer of 1864 Parker's Hole, a deep abyss of approximately 15-20 feet, proved an unsuspected obstacle for Union soldiers retreating from the Shenandoah River's western shore to its eastern side on July 18, 1864.

➡ TO STOP 6

Return to the paved path until you notice a concrete trail moving up the slopes to your right. Take the concrete path up the slope until you reach the wayside marker near the crest. Please note that this is a somewhat steep incline so please proceed accordingly. The distance to this stop is 0.18 miles.

Stop 6 – Positions of Union Artillery

If you position yourself so that the wayside marker is behind you, the bluffs to your front and right, which is private property, were the positions of Union artillery during the battle. Battery C, 1st Rhode Island Light Artillery was positioned above you. Battery G, 1st Rhode Island Light Artillery and Battery E, 1st West Virginia Artillery, were posted on the heights to your right (south).

➡ TO STOP 7

Reverse course and proceed back to the paved path that parallels the Shenandoah River (the path you have walked on for much of this tour). Keeping the Shenandoah River on your right proceed to the area where you can view the river cutting between the two islands in the river. The distance to this stop is 0.41 miles.

Stop 7 – Picketing the Eastern Shore

During the night of July 18 and the early hours of the following day troops from the 37th Massachusetts Infantry and 2nd Rhode Island Infantry picketed here along the Shenandoah River's eastern shore and aided wounded Union soldiers to reach this side of the Shenandoah. This spot also offers a vantage point of the two islands in the middle of the Shenandoah River. Some wounded Union soldiers were left on the islands and buried there by comrades when Union forces recrossed the river on July 20, 1864.

Additional Sites of Interest

Although not in the battle's immediate vicinity these additional sites are intimately connected with the battle of Cool Spring and merit a visit.

Wickliffe Church
3568 Wickliffe Road
Berryville, VA 22611
GPS coordinates: 39.16635°N, 77.89187°W

This Episcopal Church was constructed in 1846. The church was placed on the National Register of Historic Places in 1995. Confederate troops from Maj. Gen. Robert Rodes's division encamped in the vicinity of Wickliffe Church prior to the battle of Cool Spring.

Winchester National Cemetery
401 National Avenue, Winchester, VA 22601
GPS coordinates: 39.1142°N, 78.08169°W

Among the more than 5,500 graves in the Winchester National Cemetery are the graves of fourteen Union soldiers who perished at Cool Spring. Please see the roster of Cool Spring's dead for grave locations.

Winchester National Cemetery. (jn)

Stonewall Confederate Cemetery

305 East Boscawen Street, Winchester, VA 22601
GPS coordinates: 39.18282°N, 78.15786°W
Among the 2,575 burials in the Stonewall Confederate cemetery are the graves of twenty-eight Confederates who died or were mortally wounded at Cool Spring.

Stonewall Confederate Cemetery. (jn)

Battle of Rutherford's Farm Interpretive Area

151 Market Street, Winchester, VA 22603
GPS coordinates: 39.220733°N, 78.131210°W

While much of the Rutherford's Farm battlefield has been developed, a series of interpretive waysides near the north end of the Rutherford's Crossing shopping plaza parking lot explores the fighting that occurred there on July 20, 1864.

Wayside markers interpreting the battle of Rutherford's Farm. (jn)

BATTLE OF COOL SPRING
★ ★ ★
Confederate Counterattack and Union Retreat

EARLY'S 1864 ATTACK ON WASHINGTON

Early in the evening of *July 17, 1864*, Confederate forces under Gens. Gabriel C. Wharton and Robert E. Rodes counterattacked Union Col. Joseph Thoburn's division across the Shenandoah River from where you are standing. While Rodes's men pressured Thoburn's right flank, Wharton's staged two attacks that pushed the Federals back toward the river. Union artillery fire from the high ground behind you, however, stopped the Confederate advance. An artillery duel continued into the evening, as Union forces withdrew across the river under the cover of darkness. By 9 P.M. the Battle of Cool Spring was over.

Gens. Wharton and Rodes were both native Virginians who studied civil engineering at Virginia Military Institute (VMI). After graduating from VMI in 1847, Wharton became a mining engineer in the Arizona Territory. Rodes graduated in 1848 and remained on the faculty of VMI until 1851. He then moved to Alabama to work as a railroad engineer. When the war began, both men joined the Confederate army; Wharton in his native state and Rodes in Alabama. Wharton spent most of the war in the Western Theater, while Rodes saw action throughout the east. Wharton returned to Virginia in May 1864 and joined Rodes in Gen. Robert E. Lee's Army of Northern Virginia, fighting under Gen. Jubal A. Early during the Maryland invasion and back to the Shenandoah Valley. Rodes died at the Third Battle of Winchester on September 19, 1864. Wharton survived the war, returned to his engineering career, and served in the Virginia General Assembly until his death in Radford in 1906.

View looking west, between the two islands. (jn)

Colonel Joseph Thoburn

APPENDIX B

BY JONATHAN E. TRACEY

"We had hoped up to eleven o'clock last night that there might be some mistake in Gen. Sheridan's despatch," read the pages of the *Wheeling Daily Intelligencer*, "But there is no mistake." The residents of Wheeling, West Virginia, were faced with the reality that Col. Joseph Thoburn had been mortally wounded at the battle of Cedar Creek just a few days prior. Now, his remains were on the way home. Thoburn had operated a practice as a doctor there prior to the war, and Wheeling claimed him as its own throughout the conflict. The same article proclaimed, "he was, as it were, her representative among the tried and acknowledged leaders of the war." While he is less acknowledged and well known today than he once was, Thoburn was a good commander, well loved by his troops and his hometown community.

Thoburn was born in Ireland in 1825, though his family relocated to Ohio soon after. Following his education in Columbus, Ohio, and a brief position at the Ohio Lunatic Asylum, he settled in Wheeling, then Virginia, and established a medical practice there in 1853. He had a rocky start, losing his first child to illness and seeing a slow start gathering patients. Despite his own financial situation, he often rendered care foregoing payment and served on a committee to support the poor. Nevertheless, by the coming of the Civil War his family had again grown along with his practice and his standing in the community. The thirty-six-year-old first served as surgeon with the three-month enlistees of the 1st Virginia Infantry beginning in May 1861. Engaged at the battle of Philippi, most reenlisted in the three-year 1st Virginia Infantry that fall, and Thoburn was commissioned colonel as the previous commander had been promoted to brigadier general.

Thoburn commanded the regiment at the First Battle of Kernstown on March 23, 1862. There, United States forces inflicted a rare Shenandoah Valley defeat on Confederate Maj. Gen. Thomas J. "Stonewall" Jackson. Casualties were high, and Thoburn was among the wounded. He recovered at home and returned to his regiment soon after, volunteering to bring letters and small packages to his soldiers, and served for the rest of the 1862 Valley Campaign.

Thoburn first rose to brigade command during the Second Manassas Campaign, and after distinguished service the regiment earned a brief furlough in Wheeling. At a reception in 1864, Thoburn thanked the governor and the residents for their generosity and humbly noted that he "claimed nothing for himself, but the men had endured many hardships and faced terrible dangers for which they deserved much." That spring they again ventured southward into the Shenandoah Valley, finding defeat in the New Market Campaign, victory at Piedmont, and defeat at Lynchburg. Union troops fled into West Virginia, leaving Confederates open to intrude towards Washington, DC. When they rallied in Loudoun County in July, Thoburn was raised to division command. As detailed in this volume, his command was heavily engaged at Cool Spring. They suffered another defeat at the Second Battle of Kernstown on July 24, and Thoburn narrowly avoided capture, having better luck than his first battle in that area.

On several occasions, the Wheeling community discussed rumors of Thoburn's promotion to brigadier general or outright called for it. In April 1862, the local paper declared that while there were more brigadiers than necessary, Western Virginia at that time had none and "everybody, in the ranks and out of the ranks, would be glad to see [Thoburn] get it." Especially before statehood, West Virginia lacked the political lobbying necessary to secure generalships for its officers. Years later, the paper reiterated their hope, pointing out that Thoburn had been leading large commands for months. During Thoburn's last campaign, the paper falsely reported that he had received his promotion after the Third Battle of Winchester. Thoburn bore this delay well, writing that being retained at divisional command rather than replaced when other brigadier generals transferred into the Army of the Shenandoah was "a much greater compliment than the commission." Thoburn had repeatedly been put forward for promotion by his commanders. In January 1864 he was included in a list of colonels leading brigades and personally described as "in every way worthy of a higher rank." On October 2, 1864, Thoburn was at the top of Maj. Gen. George Crook's list for promotion to brevet brigadier general. Though he had risen to command a division, Thoburn never rose above the rank of colonel.

During Maj. Gen. Philip Sheridan's 1864 Shenandoah Campaign, Thoburn led his recently enlarged division to victory at the Third Battle of Winchester on September 19 and a stunning flank march at Fisher's Hill on September 22. The army moved south, then back northward burning crops in its wake until camping along the banks of Cedar Creek south of Middletown. Thoburn again led his division into action at Hupp's Hill on October 13, and on the morning of October 19 they were the first to face a pre-dawn Confederate attack at the battle of Cedar Creek. Manning their earthworks half-asleep and half-dressed, they were quickly swept away.

During this retreat, Thoburn was mortally wounded. An officer from his staff offered one account of the event, stating that while he was disentangling wagons and facilitating the retreat through Middletown, a Confederate cavalryman dressed in a United States overcoat shot Thoburn from a close distance. He lay in a vacant lot until the battle passed by and was then taken indoors. Shot through both lungs, he lingered late into the night before passing. While his command was badly bruised and scattered from the morning, the day ended in a stunningly successful Union counterattack.

Thoburn returned to Wheeling for his final rest. His remains, as well as those of Capt. Philip Bier and Sgt. Benjamin Jenkins, lay in state in Wheeling, which was "thronged during the whole day by friends and relatives." He was buried in Mt. Wood Cemetery in an elaborate ceremony headed by the Central Union Committee, the local patriotic association. One account called it "the largest funeral procession that ever took place in Wheeling." In a letter published in the *Daily Intelligencer*, Joseph Thoburn's mother shared

Colonel Thoburn's final resting place in Mt. Wood Cemetery, Wheeling, West Virginia. (jeg)

what his wife Catherine was unable to express, deep in her own mourning process. "I am requested by Mrs. Thoburn to express to you," it began, "her heartfelt thanks for the many kind services tendered to herself in her bereavement . . . a sympathy so spontaneous, so universal, and so deep, that it has made every member of the stricken family circle to feel as if living in a city of relations."

Catherine was left to raise their children alone. Joseph M. M. Thoburn was six years old, Mary Thoburn was four, and young Jennie Thoburn was only two. Amidst the display of city-wide mourning, Catherine walked into the Ohio County Recorder's Office less than a month after Joseph's death, presented her children and sacred proof of marriage, and applied for a widow's pension. Shortly after that application, she penned a short entry in the back of Joseph's wartime journal, lamenting "With three little children of our love, I am left to mourn my great and irreparable loss. My heart is torn, and I feel that all is gone." In January 1865, she began to draw a $30 monthly payment, a sad consolation for a widow, though she later received an additional $2 monthly increase for each child under 16.

When Joseph Thoburn's remains returned home, the *Daily Intelligencer* reeled, wondering "What shall we write of him?" His community rallied at the train station when his remains arrived, spoke his praises both civil and martial, and continued to remember him in the postwar period. Ritchietown, a working-class immigrant community in South Wheeling, titled their baseball team after him soon after the war. His soldiers remembered as well, and at least three posts of the Grand Army of the Republic, a veteran's organization, bore his name. Ultimately, those who knew Thoburn chose what to write; they wrote of a generous man and skilled physician, a man who cared for his town and his soldiers, an officer who patiently did his duty despite not receiving a promotion, and a martyr who died for his cause.

JONATHAN E. TRACEY *is the historian/cultural resource manager at Cedar Creek and Belle Grove National Historical Park and a contributor to Emerging Civil War. He is the co-editor of two volumes in the Emerging Civil War 10th Anniversary Series:* Civil War Monuments and Memory *and* The Civil War and Pop Culture.

The swirling and deep water of Parker's Hole caught retreating Union soldiers off guard. (jn)

Cool Spring's Dead

APPENDIX C

When Shenandoah University acquired 195 acres of the Cool Spring battlefield from the Civil War Trust (now American Battlefield Trust) in 2013, Shenandoah University's McCormick Civil War Institute (MCWI) began the process of interpreting the site. Simultaneously, with the development of interpretive signage, walking tour, and the creation of an exhibition, MCWI began the task of identifying and researching the backgrounds of the Union and Confederate soldiers either killed or mortally wounded at the battle.

Over the course of several years, a research team consisting of some of the best students I have ever had the pleasure to teach at Shenandoah University—Jake Gabriele, Victor Herrera, Kimberly Vanscoy Oliveto, Sarah Powell, Nicole Roland, Shelby Shrader, and Steven Stabler—assisted me in identifying and researching the backgrounds of those who perished at Cool Spring. My wife, Brandy Noyalas, a social studies teacher at Daniel Morgan Middle School, offered significant aid in developing the roster of the Confederate dead.

Among the sixty-five identifiable Confederate soldiers either killed or mortally wounded at Cool Spring, the average age was twenty-seven, the same as the average age of the seventy-five Union soldiers who perished. Five Confederate soldiers killed or mortally wounded at Cool Spring either enslaved or came from families who enslaved human beings. The youngest Confederate soldier killed at Cool Spring was William A. Shofner, an eighteen-year-old private in the 53rd North Carolina who mustered into service three months prior to the battle. At age sixteen Pvt. Washington Hiatt, 15th West Virginia, was the youngest Union soldier to die at Cool Spring. Fifty-two-year-old Pvt. Peter Hersch, 54th Pennsylvania, was the oldest Union soldier killed during the fight. Corporal Louis Redmon Wells, a native of Tarboro, North Carolina, who served in the 30th North Carolina Infantry, was the oldest Confederate soldier killed at Cool Spring. Wells, aged forty-eight at the time of his death, left behind a wife and six children. Wells, based on existing evidence, was one of at least eleven Confederate soldiers killed or mortally wounded who was married and had children. Eighteen of the Union soldiers whose lives were claimed by the fighting at Cool Spring were married and had children. Six of the Union soldiers who died were immigrants—one from Canada, one from England, one from Germany, one from Scotland, and two from Ireland. One Confederate soldier was an immigrant from Scotland. While the burial locations for many of those killed or mortally wounded is not known, fourteen Union soldiers are buried in the Winchester National Cemetery. Exactly twice as many Confederates are buried in the Stonewall Confederate Cemetery in Winchester.

This roster of those killed or mortally wounded at Cool Spring serves not only as a record of the battle's grim toll, but serves as a reminder that the destruction of human life that occurred on July 17-18, 1864, dramatically altered lives for family members left behind. The roster includes information about birth (when available), enlistment date, burial location, whether the soldier was killed (k) or mortally wounded (mw), and if the soldier was married and had children. Unless specified, the soldiers on this roster were killed or mortally wounded during the fighting on July 18, 1864.

Union Dead

1st West Virginia Infantry
Private Joshua B. Lukens (k): born January 12, 1845, enlisted on September 24, 1861, buried in Greenwood Cemetery, Wheeling, West Virginia.

2nd Maryland Eastern Shore Infantry
Private Edward Bausley (k): enlisted on August 30, 1862, buried in Winchester National Cemetery, grave 3998.

Private Peter Chalron (k): born in Canada in 1835, enlisted on February 8, 1864, buried in Winchester National Cemetery, grave 4007.

4th New Jersey Infantry
Private George Lee (mw):   married with two children, enlisted on August 13, 1861, died on July 19, 1864, buried on battlefield, east side of the Shenandoah River.

Private John Price (mw): born ca. 1843, married, enlisted May 22, 1861, died July 18, 1864, burial location unknown.

4th West Virginia Infantry
Sergeant Francis Clendenin (k): born in Mason City, Virginia (later West Virginia) in 1845, enlisted on September 4, 1861, burial location unknown.

Corporal Walter Gard (k): enlisted on July 21, 1861, buried in Winchester National Cemetery, grave 3887.

Corporal George W. Houson (k): enlisted on July 8, 1861, reenlisted as veteran volunteer on January 21, 1864, burial location unknown.

Private John Kinser (k): enlisted on July 5, 1861, reenlisted as a veteran volunteer on January 1, 1864, buried in Winchester National Cemetery, grave 3696.

Private Isaac Kitterman (k): born in Jackson County, Virginia (later West Virginia) in 1839, enlisted on July 25, 1861, buried in Winchester National Cemetery, grave 3914.

Private Moses Knapp (k): born in either 1844 or 1845, enlisted on July 25, 1861, burial location unknown.

5th New York Heavy Artillery

Private William E. Barrett (k): born in Utica, New York, enlisted in 23rd New York on May 16, 1861, enlisted in 5th New York Heavy Artillery on March 24, 1862, buried in Rome Cemetery, Oneida, New York.

Private Jonathan G. Berry (k): born in Ireland in 1829, enlisted on November 25, 1863, burial location unknown.

Private James Burns (k): born ca. 1826, enlisted on January 18, 1864, married with two children, burial location unknown.

Private Charles Busch (k): enlisted on December 7, 1863, burial location unknown.

Private Charles Hugh Campbell (k): enlisted on March 24, 1864, burial location unknown.

Private Hugh Carlisle (k): enlisted on February 10, 1862, buried in Winchester National Cemetery, grave 922.

Private James Darrah (k): born in Manchester, England, in 1834, married with one child, enlisted on December 3, 1863, reported buried on the battlefield.

Corporal John F. Davis (k): born in Williamstown, Massachusetts, ca. 1838, enlisted in September 1862, burial location unknown.

Private Darius Ellis (mw): born May 27, 1843, enlisted February 18, 1864, died on October 18, 1864, in Annapolis, Maryland, buried in Hartford Mills Cemetery, Hartford Mills, New York.

Private Christopher Kenner (k): born in Germany in 1845, enlisted on June 4, 1862, burial location unknown.

Private Augustus Lampman (mw): born ca. 1841, enlisted on January 2, 1864, died on July 28, 1864, buried in Butler-Savannah Cemetery, Savannah, New York.

Private Thomas Lantry (k): born in 1821, married with two children, enlisted on March 31, 1864, burial location unknown.

Private Charles H. Mallary (k): born in Ohio in 1844, enlisted on February 11, 1864, burial location unknown.

Sergeant Alexander McClure (k): born ca. 1838, married with three children, enlisted on February 4, 1862, burial location unknown.

Private Edward Mullen (mw): born ca. 1838, enlisted on September 9, 1862, burial location unknown.

Private Lynden Parker (k): enlisted on January 5, 1864, burial location unknown.

Private Nathan B. Sauter (k): born ca. 1840, enlisted February 23, 1864, burial location unknown.

Private Abraham Sears (k): born in Rockland, New York, in 1829, enlisted on November 23, 1863, burial location unknown.

Private Jacob W. Smith (k): born in 1844, enlisted on August 26, 1862, buried in Green-Wood Cemetery, Brooklyn, New York.

Private Raymond Wade (k): born in Elmira, New York, in 1844, enlisted on October 2, 1862, burial location unknown.

Private Amos Wilcox (k): born in Steuben County, New York, ca. 1830, enlisted on March 10, 1864, burial location unknown.

10th West Virginian Infantry

Private Isaac Burkhammer (k): born ca. 1838, married, enlisted on March 1, 1862, killed on July 17, 1864, burial location unknown.

11th West Virginia Infantry

Colonel Daniel Frost (mw): born in Saint Clairsville, Ohio, February 23, 1819, married with four children, commissioned lieutenant colonel May 24, 1862, brigade command at Cool Spring, died July 19, 1864, buried Mount Wood Cemetery, Wheeling, West Virginia.

Corporal Benjamin F. Jones (k): born in Marion County, Virginia (later West Virginia) in 1843, married with one child, enlisted August 31, 1862, reported buried on the battlefield.

Private Joseph McClintock (k): born in Ohio County, Virginia (later West Virginia) in 1834, enlisted August 18, 1862, burial location unknown.

15th New Jersey Infantry

Corporal Watson Chambers (mw): married with one child, enlisted in 3rd New Jersey Infantry on May 27, 1861, transferred to 15th New Jersey Infantry on June 4, 1864, died July 21, 1864, burial location unknown.

15th West Virginia Infantry

Private Robert Bell (mw): enlisted on March 29, 1864, died on August 26, 1864, at hospital in Frederick, Maryland, buried Antietam National Cemetery, grave 2622.

Private John Cunningham (k): born in Scotland in 1844, enlisted on August 23, 1862, burial location unknown.

Private Washington Hiatt (k): born in Hampshire County, Virginia (later West Virginia) in 1848, enlisted on March 31, 1864, burial location unknown, remains believed to be at the bottom of the Shenandoah River.

Private Christian Feather Lewis (k): born circa 1836, enlisted on September 1, 1862, married with three children, burial location unknown.

Lieutenant Colonel Thomas Morris (k): married with five children, commissioned captain Co. B, 7th West Virginia on October 7, 1861, commissioned lieutenant colonel 15th West Virginia on December 4, 1862, buried in Winchester National Cemetery, grave 3905.

Lieutenant Colonel Thomas Morris's grave in the Winchester National Cemetery. (jn)

18th Connecticut Infantry
Sergeant Thomas J. Aldrich (k): born in Brooklyn, Connecticut, in 1824, married with two children, buried in West Thompson Cemetery, Thompson, Connecticut.

Private John Carney (k): enlisted on August 9, 1862, burial location unknown.

Private John Delaney (k): enlisted on July 14, 1862, burial location unknown.

Corporal Gabriel Hartford (k): married with one child, enlisted on July 18, 1862, buried in Westminster Cemetery, Canterbury, Connecticut.

Private James Smith (k): born ca. 1840, enlisted on August 9, 1862, buried Smith Family Cemetery, East Killingly, Connecticut.

Private Marcus J. Weeks (k): married with one child, enlisted August 4, 1862, burial location unknown.

22nd Pennsylvania Cavalry
Private John Sanders (mw): enlisted March 30, 1864, mortally wounded on July 17, 1864, died on July 25, 1864, burial location unknown.

34th Massachusetts Infantry
Private Edwin W. Barlow (k): born ca. 1844, enlisted on July 21, 1862, buried in Winchester National Cemetery, grave 3716.

Private Dwight Chickering was one of three soldiers from the 34th Massachusetts Infantry killed at Cool Spring. (hs)

Private Dwight Chickering (k): born in Pomfret, Connecticut, in 1843, enlisted on July 17, 1862, buried Old Spencer Cemetery, Spencer, Massachusetts.

Private David F. Coats (k): enlisted on December 30, 1863, burial location unknown.

54th Pennsylvania Infantry
Private Henry Druckemiller (k): enlisted on December 13, 1861, burial location unknown.

Private Joseph Francis (k): married with two children, enlisted on June 14, 1861, burial location unknown.

Private William Henry (k): married with two children, enlisted on January 1, 1864, burial location unknown.

Private Peter Hersch, buried in the Winchester National Cemetery grave 660, was the oldest Union soldier killed at the battle. Hersch was fifty-two-years-old. (jn)

Private Peter Hersch (k): born ca. 1809, married with three children, enlisted on February 27, 1862, buried Winchester National Cemetery, grave 660.

Private Demetrius A. Holder (k): born in 1842, enlisted on January 1, 1864, burial location unknown.

Private Edward J. Lohr (mw): born in 1841, enlisted on February 1, 1862, died on August 9, 1864, at hospital in Frederick, Maryland, buried Slick Cemetery, Shade Township, Pennsylvania.

Private George Noble (k): born in County Derry, Ireland, married with one child, enlisted in 3rd Pennsylvania Reserve on September 16, 1862, transferred to 54th Pennsylvania on July 4, 1864, burial location unknown.

Second Lieutenant Ransom Griffin, 116th Ohio, completed this claim for guardianship to help Mary Farley, the four-year-old daughter of Private Joshua Farley, orphaned because of Private Farley's death at Cool Spring, obtain a pension. Mary's mother died on March 22, 1862. (na)

[Published by ROBERT CLARKE & CO., Law Publishers, 55 West Fourth St., Cincinnati.]

Claim of Guardian of Orphan Children for Pension.

The State of *Ohio*, County of *Meigs*, ss.

On this *23d* day of *August*, A. D. 18*65* before me, *A B Donnelly Clerk* of the *Court of Common Pleas* in and for the County and State above named, personally appeared *Ransom Griffin*, a resident of *Salisbury Township*, in the County of *Meigs* and State of *Ohio*, aged *27* years, who being first duly sworn according to law, doth on oath make the following declaration as guardian of the minor child of *Joshua Farley*, deceased, in order to obtain the benefits of the provision made by the Act of Congress approved July 14, 1862, granting pensions to minor children under sixteen years of age of deceased officers and soldiers:

That he is the guardian of *Mary E Farley aged four years on the 30th of August 1864*, whose father was a *Private* in Company (*G*) commanded by Captain *Hamilton L Karr*, in the *116th* Regiment of *Ohio* Volunteers, in the war of 1861, and that the said *Joshua Farley* died at *Snickers Gap Va* on or about the *18th* day of *July* 1864 by reason of *Gun Shot Wound received in action*. That the mother of the aforesaid child *Died on the 22d day of March 1862 in Salisbury Township Meigs County Ohio*

that the date of birth of his said ward *is* as follows: *Mary E Farley was born on the 30th day of August 1860*

He further declares that the parents of his said ward were married at *Rutland Meigs County Ohio*, on the *15th* day of *October* 18*57*, by *Joel P Higley a Justice of the Peace*; and he also declares that he has not in any manner been engaged in, or aided or abetted the Rebellion in the United States.

116th Ohio Infantry

Private Joshua Farley (k): born ca. 1839, married with one child, enlisted August 15, 1862, buried Winchester National Cemetery, grave 709.

Private Samuel Hayes (k): born in Marietta, Ohio, in 1845, enlisted on December 25, 1863, buried in Oak Grove Cemetery, Marietta, Ohio.

Private George Lamp (k): born ca. 1844, enlisted August 20, 1862, buried Winchester National Cemetery, grave 349.

Private William Stoneman (k): born ca. 1844, enlisted on August 22, 1862, buried Winchester National Cemetery, grave 699.

123rd Ohio Infantry

Private Lafayette Dunn (k): born ca. 1844, enlisted on August 19, 1862, burial location unknown.

Private Albert Ott (k): born ca. 1841, enlisted August 14, 1862, burial location unknown.

Private Bower W. Schnebly (k): born ca. 1841, enlisted August 17, 1862, burial location unknown.

Private Harvey Stansberry (k): born ca. 1835, enlisted August 15, 1862, buried Winchester National Cemetery, unknown grave.

Sergeant David Terry (mw): born in Marseilles, Ohio, 1835, married with two children, enlisted on August 12, 1862, died on Parker's Island at some point between July 18-20, 1864, reportedly buried on Parker's Island.

Modern-day view of Parker's Island where Sgt. David Terry, 123rd Ohio, breathed his last. (jn)

Private Lewis White (k): born in Huron County, Ohio, in 1839, married, enlisted on August 13, 1862, buried in Steuben, Ohio.

First Lieutenant Caleb D. Williams (k): born ca. 1830, married with one child, enlisted September 1, 1863, buried Riverside Cemetery, Monroeville, Ohio.

170th Ohio Infantry
Private George Harper (k): born in Harrison County, Ohio, ca. 1845, enlisted on May 2, 1864, buried Winchester National Cemetery, unknown grave.

Private James Haverfield (k): born ca. 1837, enlisted on May 2, 1864, buried "in a small garden" on east side of Shenandoah River.

Colonel Samuel Young's Dismounted Cavalry
Private William Cushman, 2nd Ohio Cavalry (k): born ca. 1833, married, enlisted August 24, 1861, buried Winchester National Cemetery, grave 692.

1st Massachusetts Cavalry
Sergeant William McKinney, (k): born in Readville, Massachusetts in 1839, enlisted on January 5, 1864, burial location unknown.

5th United States Cavalry
Private William Wright (k): married, enlisted on March 11, 1864, burial location unknown.

Confederate Dead

2nd North Carolina Infantry
Private Adam Hartman (mw): born ca. 1821, married with four children, enlisted on September 27, 1863, died at Mount Jackson, Virginia, on undeterminable date, burial location unknown.

Corporal Henry J. Jones (mw): born in Wilson County, North Carolina, on January 12, 1840, enlisted July 18, 1861, died on July 22, 1864, buried Stonewall Confederate Cemetery, Winchester, Virginia.

Lieutenant Colonel Walter Stallings (k): born ca. 1834, enlisted on May 16, 1861, buried Stonewall Confederate Cemetery, Winchester, Virginia.

2nd North Carolina Infantry Battalion

Sergeant William D. Craven (mw): born ca. 1843, enlisted September 19, 1862, died at General Hospital in Winchester, Virginia, July 26, 1864, buried Stonewall Confederate Cemetery, Winchester, Virginia.

Private Martin Meese (mw): enlisted June 28, 1864, buried Stonewall Confederate Cemetery, Winchester, Virginia.

Sergeant Aaron Pickard (mw): born ca. 1843, enlisted September 1861, died July 19, 1864, burial location unknown.

4th North Carolina Infantry

Private David S. Bustle (k): born ca. 1840, enlisted June 7, 1861, buried Stonewall Confederate Cemetery, Winchester, Virginia.

Private Arthur Evans (k): married with one child, enlisted April 18, 1862, buried Evans Family Cemetery, Wilson, North Carolina.

Private Martin Snow (k): enlisted May 29, 1861, burial location unknown.

Colonel James Hall Wood (k): born ca. 1840, enlisted May 16, 1861, buried Third Creek Presbyterian Church Cemetery, Rowan, North Carolina.

5th Alabama Infantry

Private S.R. Burnett (mw): died at the General Hospital in Winchester, Virginia, July 21, 1864, burial location unknown.

Private George W. Prude (k): born ca. 1843, enlisted April 20, 1861, buried Stonewall Confederate Cemetery, Winchester, Virginia.

Private Daniel C. Rankin (k): enlisted July 29, 1861, buried Stonewall Confederate Cemetery, Winchester, Virginia.

6th Alabama Infantry

Private Elkanah G. Arant (mw): born ca. 1845, enlisted on March 1, 1862, died on July 21, 1864, buried Stonewall Confederate Cemetery, Winchester, Virginia.

9th Louisiana Infantry

Captain Reuben Allen Pierson (k): born in Stewart County, Georgia, September 23, 1834, enlisted July 7, 1861, buried Stonewall Confederate Cemetery, Winchester, Virginia.

The Louisiana section of the Stonewall Confederate Cemetery contains the graves of seventy Louisianians. Captain Reuben Allen Pierson is among them. Pierson's tombstone, illegible today, is situated to the right of the Louisiana monument. (jn)

12th Alabama Infantry
Private John T. Eberhart (k): enlisted March 2, 1863, burial location unknown.

Lieutenant Alexander Majors (k): enlisted on June 13, 1861, believed to be buried in unmarked grave, Stonewall Confederate Cemetery, Winchester, Virginia.

Private G.W. Parnell (mw): died at the General Hospital in Winchester, Virginia, July 21, 1864, buried Stonewall Confederate Cemetery, Winchester, Virginia, in grave marked "G.R. Purnell."

Private Jasper West (mw): died at the General Hospital in Winchester, Virginia, July 23, 1864, buried Stonewall Confederate Cemetery, Winchester, Virginia, in grave erroneously marked "Joseph West."

12th Georgia Infantry
Lieutenant William F. Lowe (k): enlisted on June 11, 1861, burial location unknown.

21st Georgia Infantry
Private Samuel Godwin (k): enlisted October 23, 1863, burial location unknown.

26th Georgia Infantry
Private David J. Hickox (k): enlisted in 3rd Georgia Infantry on March 1, 1862, transferred to 26th Georgia Infantry on April 10, 1863, buried Stonewall Confederate Cemetery, Winchester, Virginia.

Sergeant Stephen W. Myers (mw): enlisted May 4, 1861, died July 20, 1864, burial location unknown.

Sergeant Bryant Sweat (mw): born in Ware County, Georgia, in 1839, enlisted April 18, 1861, died at the General Hospital in Winchester, Virginia, July 21, 1864, buried Stonewall Confederate Cemetery, Winchester, Virginia.

30th North Carolina Infantry
Private Arkin B. Bell (k): born in 1835, enlisted March 10, 1862, burial location unknown.

Sergeant John N. Black (k): born ca. 1834, enlisted September 13, 1861, burial location unknown.

Private Elijah Crotts (k): born in 1822, married, burial location unknown.

Sergeant Aaron Leondias DeArmond (mw): born in Mecklenburg, North Carolina, February 12, 1827, married with five children, enlisted September 13, 1861, died on August 19, 1864, buried in Sardis Presbyterian Church Cemetery, Charlotte, North Carolina.

Corporal Richard Felton (k): born ca. 1832, enlisted August 31, 1862, burial location unknown.

Private Thomas Gupton (k): born ca. 1840, enlisted on September 10, 1861, burial location unknown.

Sergeant James W. Teachey (k): born ca. 1838, married, enlisted August 28, 1861, burial location unknown.

Private Jacob Teachey (mw): born ca. 1843, enlisted March 3, 1862, died January 17, 1865, burial location unknown.

Corporal Lewis Redmon Wells (mw): born ca. 1815, married with six children, enlisted August 13, 1861, died July 21, 1864, burial location unknown.

32nd North Carolina Infantry

Private Nicholas G. Long (k): born in Mississippi in 1839, enlisted in 15th North Carolina Infantry on May 20, 1861, transferred to 32nd North Carolina Infantry on July 4, 1862, burial location unknown.

Captain Gilbert M. Sherrill (mw): born in Newtown, North Carolina, on July 4, 1837, died at the General Hospital in Winchester, Virginia, July 24, 1864, buried Stonewall Confederate Cemetery, Winchester, Virginia.

36th Virginia Infantry

Sergeant John T. Kimberling (k): born ca. 1841, enlisted May 3, 1862, buried Stonewall Confederate Cemetery, Winchester, Virginia.

Private John T. Meadows (k): enlisted on December 10, 1862, buried Stonewall Confederate Cemetery, Winchester, Virginia, in grave marked "J. B. Meadows."

38th Georgia Infantry

Sergeant Andrew Jackson "Jack" Williamson, Jr. (k): born in Montgomery County, Georgia, in 1842, enlisted October 1, 1861, buried Stonewall Confederate Cemetery, Winchester, Virginia.

43rd North Carolina Infantry

Lieutenant William Beavans (mw): enlisted in 1st North Carolina Infantry April 27, 1861, enlisted in 43rd North Carolina Infantry, February 25, 1862, died July 31, 1864, buried Stonewall Confederate Cemetery, Winchester, Virginia.

William Beavans's tombstone in the Stonewall Confederate Cemetery in Winchester, Virginia. (jn)

Sergeant Marmaduke Bell (k): born ca. 1836, married with three children, buried Lawrence Cemetery, Edgecombe County, North Carolina.

Private Charles M. Bullard (k): enlisted April 4, 1864, burial location unknown.

Private Illy N. Dicken (k): born ca. 1830, enlisted February 11, 1862, burial location unknown.

Private Edmund Jacob Dickins (k): born ca. 1835, married with three children, burial location unknown.

Lieutenant Stephen W. Ellerbe (mw): born ca. 1838, married with two children, enlisted May 9, 1862, died at the General Hospital in Winchester, Virginia, July 31, 1864, buried Stonewall Confederate Cemetery, Winchester, Virginia, in grave marked "S.W. Elberb."

Private Henry T. Jones (k): enlisted May 16, 1862, burial location unknown.

Private William Eli Lewis (k): born ca. 1838, enlisted February 12, 1862, burial location unknown.

Corporal Elish Dargan E.D. Liles (k): born in Anson County, North Carolina, on February 23, 1841, enlisted on February 25, 1862, buried Stonewall Confederate Cemetery, Winchester, Virginia.

Private James W. Loften (k): enlisted on November 23, 1863, burial location unknown.

Lieutenant Jesse Macon (mw): born ca. 1838 in Halifax County, North Carolina, enlisted in 15th Mississippi Infantry on May 8, 1862, transferred to 43rd North Carolina Infantry in March 1863, died on August 24, 1864, buried Alston Cemetery, Halifax County, North Carolina.

Private John A. Pairman (k): born ca. 1829 in Lanarkshire, Scotland, married with one child, enlisted February 10, 1862, burial location unknown.

Corporal Andrew Parks (k): born ca. 1825, married with two children, enlisted February 3, 1862, burial location unknown.

Corporal Joseph W. Phifer (k): born ca. 1839, enlisted February 25, 1862, burial location unknown.

Private William J. Smith (k): born ca. 1845, enlisted on May 2, 1862, burial location unknown.

Private John Stearns (k): born ca. 1831, married with three children, enlisted April 2, 1862, burial location unknown.

Private John H. Outlaw (k): enlisted on April 22, 1862, burial location unknown.

Private Thomas B. Harrington (mw): enlisted on January 7, 1864, died July 25 1864, buried Stonewall Confederate Cemetery, Winchester, Virginia.

43rd Tennessee Infantry (Vaughn's Brigade)
Private Samuel Hugh Vincent (k): married with six children, enlisted on November 1, 1861, buried Stonewall Confederate Cemetery, Winchester, Virginia.

51st Virginia Infantry
Private Lemuel Allen (k): born ca. 1839, married with one child, enlisted July 31, 1861, buried Stonewall Confederate Cemetery, Winchester, Virginia, in grave marked "Pvt Samuel Allen."

53rd North Carolina Infantry
Sergeant John F. Collins (mw): born ca. 1839, enlisted June 23, 1862, buried Stonewall Confederate Cemetery, Winchester, Virginia, in grave marked "S. F. Collins."

Colonel William Allison Owen (mw): born September 19, 1833, married, commissioned first lieutenant April 16, 1861, 1st North Carolina Infantry, commissioned major 34th North Carolina Infantry on January 28, 1862, commissioned lieutenant colonel 11th North Carolina Infantry on March 31, 1862, commissioned colonel 53rd North Carolina Infantry, May 6, 1862, died July 19, 1864, buried Old Settlers Cemetery, Charlotte, North Carolina.

Private William A. Shofner (mw): born ca. 1846, enlisted April 18, 1864, died July 27, 1864, burial location unknown.

54th North Carolina Infantry
Sergeant William B. Morrison (mw): born ca. 1844, enlisted April 28, 1862, died at the General Hospital in Winchester, Virginia, July 21, 1864, buried Stonewall Confederate Cemetery, Winchester, Virginia, in grave marked "W.E. Morrison."

60th Virginia Infantry
Private Haywood Hodge (mw): born ca. 1839, enlisted on July 4, 1861, died at the General Hospital in Winchester, Virginia, July 20, 1864, buried Stonewall Confederate Cemetery, Winchester, Virginia.

61st Alabama Infantry
Private Robert Caswell Ellington (mw): born in Georgia on December 10, 1845, enlisted September 1, 1863, died July 19, 1864, buried Stonewall Confederate Cemetery, Winchester, Virginia.

Thomas' Legion (North Carolina)
Private John A. Beck (mw): enlisted July 19, 1862, died on July 19, 1864, buried Stonewall Confederate Cemetery, Winchester, Virginia.

*   *   *

The information contained on this roster is derived from Jake Gabriele, Victor Herrera, Jonathan A. Noyalas, Sarah Powell, & Shelby R. Shrader, "'The Shenandoah Chanting Its Endless Requiem': A Roster of Cool Spring's Union Dead," *Journal of the Shenandoah Valley during the Civil War Era* 3 (2020): 3-29; Jake Gabriele, Victor Herrera, Brandy N. Noyalas, Jonathan A. Noyalas, Kimberley Vanscoy Oliveto, Nicole A. Roland, Shelby R. Shrader, and Steven Stabler, "'Life was Extinct': A Roster of Cool Spring's Confederate Dead," *Journal of the Shenandoah Valley during the Civil War Era* 4 (2021): 3-34.

The final resting place of the unknown Confederate dead removed from the Cool Spring battlefield is marked by this stone in the Stonewall Confederate Cemetery. (jn)

View of the Shenandoah River looking north. (jn)

"A Christopher of the Shenandoah"

APPENDIX D

In 1893 poet Edith M. Thomas, a native of Ohio who was nine years old at the time of the battle of Cool Spring, published the poem "A Christopher of the Shenandoah: Island Ford, Snicker's Gap, July 18, 1864" as part of a poetry collection called *Fair Shadow Land*. Although it is unclear what motivated Thomas to craft the poem, it focuses on the heroic efforts to evacuate wounded Union soldiers from the eastern side of the Shenandoah River to the western side, property which today is owned by Shenandoah University. Although largely forgotten today the poem, according to newspaper coverage of Memorial Day ceremonies in the late 1800s and early 1900s, was a mainstay of programs. At the time of her death in 1925 Thomas was lauded as one of a "few American poets who have come nearer to affording examples of the perfection of form, as the rules of poetry were understood in the nineteenth century."

Poet Edith M. Thomas (al)

A CHRISTOPHER OF THE SHENANDOAH

ISLAND FORD, SNICKER'S GAP, JULY 18,1864

TOLD BY THE ORDERLY

BY EDITH M. THOMAS

Mute he sat in the saddle—mute midst our full
    acclaim,
As three times over we gave to the mountain
echo his name.
Then, "But I couldn't do less!" in a murmur
    remonstrant came

This was the deed his spirit set and his hand
    would not shun,
When the vale of the Shenandoah had lost the
    glow of the sun,
And the evening cloud and the battle smoke were
    blending in one.

Retreating and ever retreating, the bank of the
    river we gained,
Hope of the field was none, and choice but of
    flight remained,
When there at the brink of the ford his horse he
    Suddenly reined.

For his vigilant eye had marked where, close by
    the oozy marge,
Half-parted its moorings, there lay a battered
    and oarless barge.
"Quick! gather the wounded in!" and they flying
    stayed at his charge.

They gathered the wounded in whence they fell
    by the river bank,
Lapped on the gleaming sand, or aswoon, 'mid
    the rushes dank;
And they crowded the barge till its sides low
    down in the water sank.

The river was wide, was deep, and heady the
    current flowed,
A burdened and oarless craft!—straight into
    the stream he rode
By the side of the barge, and drew it along with
    its moaning load.
A moaning and ghastly load—the wounded—
    the dying—the dead!
Our bravest the mark, yet unscathed and un-
    daunted, he pushed ahead.

Alone? Save for one that from love of his
    leader or soldierly pride
(Hearing his call for aid, and seeing that none
    Replied),
Plunged and swam by the crazy craft on the
    other side.

But Heaven! what weary toil! for the river is
    wide, is deep;
The current is swift, and the bank on the further
    side is steep.
'T is reached at last, and a hundred of ours to
    the rescue leap.

Oh, they cheered as he rose from the stream and
    the water-drops flowed away!
"But I couldn't do less!" in the silence that fol-
    lowed we heard him say;
Then the wounded cheered, and the swooning
    awoke in the barge where they lay.

And I?—Ah, well, I swam by the barge on the
    other side;
But an orderly goes wherever his leader chooses
    to ride.
Come life or come death I couldn't do less than
    follow his guide.

Troops from the 37th Massachusetts and 2nd Rhode Island picketed this area along the east side of the Shenandoah River. (jn)

When a University Takes Stewardship of a Battlefield

APPENDIX E

In 2013, the Civil War Trust (now American Battlefield Trust) purchased 195 acres of the Cool Spring Battlefield situated on the east bank of the Shenandoah River. The Trust transferred stewardship of the land to Shenandoah University that same year with the understanding that the site would be utilized as an experiential classroom—one that would educate Shenandoah students in the fields of history and environmental studies. Since Shenandoah University received the awesome task of managing this portion of the Cool Spring Battlefield, Shenandoah University's McCormick Civil War Institute (MCWI) has assumed the responsibility of crafting interpretation at the site and developing an array of educational programs for students of all ages.

Since the establishment of Shenandoah University's River Campus at Cool Spring Battlefield in 2013, students in Civil War Era Studies, under my direction, have played a significant part in interpreting the site. An exhibition about the battle located in the Lodge, which includes an array of artifacts, an interpretive video about the site available online at https://www.su.edu/mcwi/touring-the-battle-of-cool-spring/, walking tour guide, handout about the experiences of enslaved people, and augmented reality experiences have all been developed with the aid of Shenandoah University's students. The site has truly proved a laboratory for students to hone their research and public history skills.

Each year, Shenandoah University's River Campus at Cool Spring Battlefield, maintained by a small staff with support from a cadre of volunteers during the summer, welcomes thousands of visitors from across the world who visit to explore the site's rich history and contemplate the Civil War's tragic consequences.

Shenandoah University's River Campus at Cool Spring Battlefield is open year-round, sunrise to sunset.

Although covered in trees today, at the time of the battle, Parker's Island contained few trees. (jn)

Select Accounts from Soldiers Who Fought at Cool Spring

APPENDIX F

Letter from Private William McMurphy to Mother
(Author's Collection)

William Otis McMurphy, 7th Michigan Cavalry, was one of the dismounted troopers in Col. Samuel Young's command. On July 17, 1864, McMurphy, who served in the 1st Michigan Infantry earlier in the conflict, wrote his mother about the hardships of the march from the nation's capital and how he looked forward to the looming battle.

Camp in the Field Near Percersvile [Purcellville] Va
July 17th 1864

Dear Mother

I now will proceed to inform you of my whereabouts. We are still following up the Rebs and are near Snickers Gap and expect to march tonight or in the morning. The Rebs have caught particular thunder for the last few days. We have captured a large wagon train and a good many Prisoners and expect to capture a good many more. I have stood it so far first rate but don't know how long I can march if we make long marches. I hope we can whip the Rebs this summer for I am getting sick of soldiering. My feet are one mass of blisters but the hopes of using up the Johnnys this summer is good as a plaster for my feet you will probably not get a letter from me again very soon and I don't know as this will go. There is a report that we will get horses. I hope so for then we can go in on the Big Side. I don't know what the Reason is but every time I think of going into a fight I feel Bully just as though we were sure of whipping them. It is so dark that I can't see where I am writing. Give my best to respects to everybody and accept my love for yourself.

Good Bye
Wm McMurphy

P.S. Direct your letters just the same and keep writing

Captain John Chamberlin to Mary Ann Terry
(Widows Pension File, National Archives and Records Administration)

Three days after the battle of Cool Spring Capt. John Chamberlin, 123rd Ohio Infantry, performed the unpleasant task of writing Sgt. David Terry's wife, Mary Ann, that Terry died from wounds received during the battle. Chamberlin's detailed letter is the first of five letters included in this appendix that appear in the widow's pension files at the National Archives and Records Administration, further attesting to their enormous value.

Camp of the 123d O.V.I.
Near Snicker's Gap, Va. 21st
July 1864

Mrs. D.D. Terry

Dear Madam

It becomes my unpleasant duty this morning to communicate to you sad tidings. Monday afternoon our force reached the bank of the Shenandoah river, found the Rebels on the opposite side. Our Brigade was immediately deployed as skirmishers, soon driving the Rebels from the bank. We waded the river—which is about 15 rods wide at that place with quite a large island in it and took up our position on this side. The left wing of the 123d was sent out as skirmishers. Col. Wilson being in command of them. A general engagement coming on we were moved down on the right where we also became engaged. Here Stansberry Anderson & John Davis were wounded. The force on the right was ordered to fall back across the river, after we had got to the edge of the river we (123d) again rallied and formed on the bank. Just at this time I noticed a man in the corner of the fence about 20 feet in advance of ours with his face to the enemy, who were only about 100 yds. in front of us. I saw him struck, but not seeing his face, supposed him to belong to some other Regt. but after we recrossed the river, which we done immediately, I learned that it was your husband. He was carried off by two men of our Regt onto the island & left there with other wounded men it being impossible at that time to take them any further. Next day the Rebels held possession of the river bank & it was impossible to get to the island. Yesterday afternoon, we crossed the river again and went into camp near the battlefield. Immediately afterwards, not being allowed to go myself I sent several men to search for David & John Anderson. They found your husband's body buried on the island near where he had been laid. We had it taken up and reburied on the island. We could not procure any coffin, but his shirt, pants, & socks were on, and wrapping him in a blanket, they reinterred him the best they could placing a board at the head, with his name & Regiment on it. They also discovered his watch concealed under a log within reach of where he lay and where he had undoubtedly placed it. There was nothing in his pockets. He was struck by a musket ball in the left breast just below the nipple and could have survived but a very short time. I have his watch & a lock of his hair, which I will send to you by express to Upper Sandusky, the first opportunity. Thus has another brave soldier gone to his final rest. There never was a braver or truer soldier than your husband. In camp he always knew his duty and performed it well. It time of action he was always cool and collected, foremost in daring, and knew no such thing as fear.

At the time of his death he was the only sergeant in the company and was acting as orderly & next to me had charge of the company. He was well known throughout the regiment and highly respected by both officers and men, all of whom sympathize with you in this your deep affliction. But human sympathy avails little. You must look to him "who is a husband to the widow and a father to the orphan" for strength and support in this your time of great need. Believe me when I say I have felt his loss more deeply than that of any other man. His occupying the position he did brought him into closer contact with me than any other man of the company. It at any time I can be of any service to you, do not hesitate to call upon me.

Sympathizing with you, believe me.
Your sincere friend,

J.W Chamberlin
Capt. Co. A 123d O.V.I.

Assistant Surgeon William Henry Harrison Cobb to Unknown (*The Daily Confederate*, Raleigh, NC)

Three days after the battle William Henry Harrison Cobb, the 2nd North Carolina Infantry's assistant surgeon, wrote a "private letter" about the battle. Nine days later *The Daily Confederate*, a newspaper in Raleigh, North Carolina, published the letter's contents.

July 21st 1864

On the 18th instant while resting in camp, eight miles from Charlestown and four miles from Castleman's or Snicker's Ferry, we received orders to move out, and the column took up line of march towards the ferry, where a large force of the enemy, consisting of Hunter's command, the 6th Corps and some heavy artillery converted into infantry, had crossed and were skirmishing with our cavalry. We formed a line of battle, deployed the sharpshooters of the division (Rodes) command by Col. Brown of the 1st North Carolina Infantry, who had just returned from a wounded furlough. About half pat four, p.m., an advance was ordered; the enemy were engaged and a severe fight ensued. I can not speak of the exploits of the entire division. Grimes' brigade, commanded by Col. Owens, of the 53d North Carolina troops, who joined his command from a wounded furlough that day, engaged the enemy, who were posted behind a rock fence, and Cox's brigade was sent around to flank them, which they did handsomely, killing and wounding a great many, throwing them into confusion, and making them retire to the river. We drove some of them into the river and drowned many of them. The enemy had several batteries placed upon the mountains, over the river, and shelled our forces terribly, but the column being in motion, kept out of range. We were unable, however, to hold the river bank, so after getting all the wounded off the field, we retired that night about half a mile to bivouac and await the movements of the enemy in the morning. The 2d regiment was in the hottest of the fray, with the remnants of the 1st and 3d which were consolidated under the command of Col. Thruston. The 14th was on picket towards Harpers Ferry, and was thus fortunate enough to miss the engagement. The loss of the 2d was heavier than any other. I append a list of the killed and wounded. The loss of our brigade in field officers was heavy. Besides Col. Stallings of the 2d, we have to mourn the loss of Col. Wood of the 4th and Col. Owens of the 53d, commanding Grimes' brigade.

Lieutenant Colonel Elijah Massey to Colonel Joseph Thoburn (Compiled Service Record, National Archives and Records Administration)

It is always useful to be mindful of the physical toll that marching and the natural environment exacted on soldiers. Three days after the battle of Cool Spring, Lt. Col. Elijah Massey, 2nd Maryland Eastern Shore, shared how campaigning that summer adversely affected him and appealed to his superior for a furlough.

HeadQuarters 2nd E.S. Maryland Vols. Inf.
In Camp Near Snickers Ford Va.
July 21, 1864
Col. Thoburn
Com'g 1st Div. Dept. W.Va.

Sir,

I most earnestly apply to you for a sick leave of absence for thirty days or even for a less time, for the following reason viz. From the sever exposure during our long march to Lynchburg and ack my physical strength has become entirely exhausted and from the effects of fording the Shenandoah River on the 18th inst. I am much worse. A disease of the kidneys & bladder which has come on me during the year past is now so much increased that I cannot urinate only by drops. I have been in the service three years the 2nd day of October next and have had but one furlough for 15 days and have never been on the sick list before.

I have no doubt that my health can be in a short time completely restored, provided I can get to my family for a short time. The field officers of the Regiment are all Present. The surgeon certificate will accompany this application.

Very respectfully
Your obdt. Servant
E.E. Massey
Lt. Col. 2 E.S. Md Vols. Infy.

Captain Robert S. Johnston to Henry M. Lee
(Widows Pension File, National Archives and Records Administration)

Private Henry Lee, 4th New Jersey Infantry, was among a handful of soldiers from Maj. Gen. Horatio Wright's Sixth Corps who perished at Cool Spring. Six days after the battle Capt. Robert S. Johnston shared the unfortunate news with Lee's father, Henry.

Camp of the 4th N.J. Vols.
July 24th 1864

Henry M. Lee

Dear Sir,

I am embrace the present time to inform you of the death of your son "George" who was mortally wounded on the 18th inst. About eight o'clock by a shell from one of the enemy's battery's. He was struck in the arm cutting through the bone in two about the elbow joing and making three severe cuts in his head, one in the chin, one on the left face & one directly under the left eye all of these were about two inches in length. He lived until the following day died at four o'clock. He suffered severely from pain was unconscious during the day. I saw him breath his last, stood over him for some time so as to [be] able to inform you of the fact. He was buried in a box made for him between Snickers Gap and the Shenandoah River, under a tree with a head board to mark the place, put well in the ground to keep it in its place. The place is about one half mile from the gap. His watch and pocket book was taken from his pocket by the men of his Co. I will get them and express them to you. The regiment was forming near the Shenandoah just about dark when the enemy commenced shelling us or not us but a Battery in our front the shell passing over the Battery and striking in our ranks. There was three other killed and three severely wounded. The chaplain of the 15th Regt. officiated at his burial.

Give my respects to Charles and adieu from your friend.

R.S. Johnston
Capt. Co. B 4th N.J. Vols.

Private J. A. Blackmon to Mary Darrah
(Widows Pension File, National Archives and Records Administration)

No single Union regiment engaged at Cool.Spring suffered more casualties than the 5th New York Heavy Artillery. Pvt. James Darrah was among those killed. One week after the battle Darrah's comrade, Pvt. J.A. Blackmon, described the circumstances of Darrah's death and explained the financial benefits to which her husband's death entitled her.

Harpers Ferry W.Va
July 25th 1864

Mrs. Darrah

I have sad news to communicate. Your husband James Darrah C. Co. 5th Artillery N.Y. Vols. was shot through the head at the battle of Snickers Gap July 18th and killed instantly. I write you this thinking you may not have been informed of the fact as I have seen no list of the killed in the papers and as his captain and comrades have not been very favorably situated to report casualties. The news comes to me from 3 or 4 different members of the Company who were present at the battle and who have informed that they knew positively that he was killed in the manner above mentioned and that they saw the place where he was buried. So I fear the report is only too true.

Your husband enlisted in the regiment at the same time I did and although we were in different companies I knew him and esteemed him highly as an honorable patriot & companion in arms, and the news of his death could hardly grieve me more were I a near and dear relative. You can learn more of particulars probably by applying to Captain H.L. Emmons who is yet with his Company. I believe there is due your husband pay for the month of May, June and July up to the day of his death and Government Bounty to the *amount of $200. I am not positive as to whether the State of N.Y. bounty was ever paid him, but think it was. This money can be collected if the proper steps are taken in time. Wishing you all possible consolation in this great affliction.*

I am yours respectfully
J.A. Blackmon
Private H Co. 5th Artillery N.Y. Vols.

Unidentified Soldier from North Carolina to Raleigh Confederate (*Fayetteville Semi-Weekly Observer*, Fayetteville, NC)

On August 4, 1864, the *Fayetteville Semi-Weekly Observer* published a letter from an unknown North Carolinian. The letter details Early's movement to Snickers Gap, the clash on July 18, and the soldier's assessment of the fight.

July 27, 1864

On Saturday, July 16th, this army left its encampment near Leesburg, and took the road for Winchester by way of Snicker's Gap in the Blue Ridge. About 1 o'clock we passed the village of Purcellville, our baggage train was attacked by the enemy's cavalry. They cut out 70 wagons and ambulances, and were making off with them, when Brig. Gen. Lewis, at the head of our brigade, reached the ground and changed the aspect of affairs in double-quick time. The enemy had to abandon many of the wagons and fly for safety, leaving behind about 15 of his troopers killed and wounded on the field. We also captured from him 1 piece of artillery. Our army crossed the Blue Ridge and took position near Berryville in order to rest from its toilsome marches. On Sunday afternoon and Monday, it was apparent from the continual firing of artillery that the enemy were following us through Snicker's Gap in force—our cavalry which had been covering our rear disputing their advance. This Gap is a position easily flanked. Our cavalry fell back in the evening. In the afternoon of Monday, the 18th, the enemy advanced in force and threw a large body of troops across the Shenandoah where the Turnpike crosses. Our troops were ready to receive them. The work of sharpshooting was spirited and severe. The enemy had been enabled to form his line of battle on the north bank of the river immediately upon and under cover of the bank. This line was charged by Rodes' and a part of Gordon's divisions. The yankee line was broken, and gave way through its entire length; the fugitives plunged into the river which is here about 150 yards in width, and sought safety in this dangerous mode of retreat. Our riflemen now had a fair chance, and gave ample testimony of their competency in such bloody work. Never since the sound of the rifle was first heard in this beautiful Valley have the "sea green" waters of the Shenandoah been so reddened with human gore as on this afternoon. The water was literally covered with the fallen foe. The battle is soon over and the victory ours. The enemy's loss in killed and wounded is estimated at 1,000. But, oh! what a price is paid for it! 300 are said to be killed and wounded on our side. Cols. Owen and Wood, both of North Carolina, are reported mortally wounded, and how sad did I feel in the morning upon finding my esteemed young friend Lieut. Bivens, of Enfield, who had lost a leg in the action. But such is the fate of war.

On Tuesday the 19th, it became apparent that the enemy were threatening our position from different points, and on Wednesday morning the 20th, our army showed a disposition to fall back. The sick and wounded were sent off from Winchester to the hospitals at Mt. Jackson and Staunton.

Second Lieutenant William Byron Henry to Sister
(Author's Collection)

During the first week of August 2nd Lt. William Byron Henry, 116th Ohio Infantry, wrote his sister about events through which he passed during the previous two weeks and how the mistreatment of Pvt. Samuel Hayes by Confederates in the aftermath of Cool Spring transformed him.

Near Wolfstown, Md.
August 2d 1864

My Dear Sister,

Will you do me the favor of noticing from me a pencil traced note, which perhaps you have blamed me for not writing long time ago. The trouble has been a lack of mail communication with the rear. Twice on the raid did I write you, but each time communications were cut off and letters burned.

Since I saw you last we have marched over two hundred miles. Fought two battles and skirmished constantly. Have waded the Potomac river (waist deep) twice, the Shenandoah three times, run clear around Robin Hoods barn crossed Blue Ridge and have at last run into the passes of South Mountain and stopped near Wolfstown, Md. 10 miles southeast of Hagerstown.

At Snickers Gap we punished the enimee pretty muchly, but at Winchester we got whipped in about half of no time. In fact our Brigade (the 1st) did not get into the engagement [Second Battle of Kernstown] except a line of skirmishers, before the left was flanked (we occupied extreme right) and the whole line retired. We were outnumbered so much that we could not make another stand until we got to Bunker Hill — 12 miles above Martinsburg. I with Co. B was put out on Picket from Bunker Hill 1 ½ miles toward Winchester about 11:00 P.M. the night of after the fight 25th July. In the morning as soon as [it was] light we found ourselves close enough to the mounted reb Pickets to converse without exerting our lungs severely at all. They asked us to "surrender" to which we replied with a volley and had the pleasure to see some of them tipped out [of] their saddles. We had none hurt but came near being flanked and being cut off before we could fall back to our support. The right supposed us captured until we joined them at Williamsport, Md. the next day. I have had a fight every time we've been on picket this summer.

We fought at Snickers Ferry 18th July and although we punished the enemy severely we had taken a position we could not hold long and as soon as dark we retired acrost the river leaving our dead on the field. I had one killed carried him a mile but could not get him acrost. The third day after the fight we crossed again – had been relieved by the 6th Corps and found no rebs, our dead had been stripped by the fiends and left unburied. They robbed my little dead boy Sam[ue]l Hayes from Coalville. My determination is to retiate upon the carcasses of live rebels. Bang goes a musket followed by a groan from some poor fellow has shot himself.

8:00 P.M. The man that shot himself was a private of the 1st Va. Cav. Shot off three of his fingers. Such things are frequent in the army. Have just received orders to be ready to march at 3:00 a.m. to-morrow. Know not what direction.

Paper is almost as scarce as hard tack. Say to Aunt Rhoda that she has no idea the vast amount of comfort my "Kitt" is to me. No one but a soldier can appreciate the advantages of the "housewives" and even he must be on a raid for three months with but one suit of clothes. In it I carry all my valuab[les] commission and other papers. My load is composed of my Kitt, canteen, and sword. Have not pitched a tent for near three months. At night when I retire to my bed chamber I usually chose me the smooth place near the head of Co. B's stack of Springfields. My boots answer the purpose of a pillow. My blouse that of a blanket. I will now bring my weary wandering to a close.

Address Lt. W.B. Henry
Company "B" 116th Regt. O.V.I.
Via Parksersburg, West Va.
To Follow Reg't
Affectionately your bro,
Byron

Second Lieutenant George W. Byard to Mary Cushman (Widows Pension File, National Archives and Records Administration)

Less than one month after the battle of Cool Spring Mary Cushman, the wife of Pvt. William Cushman, 2nd Ohio Cavalry, received word of her husband's death at Cool Spring from 2nd Lt. George Byard.

Camp Stoneman, DC
August 15th 1864
Mrs. Cushman

Yours of Aug. 9th is received. In reply [I] would say that your husband Wm Cushman left the camp under my command on the 5th of July after a great deal of hard fatiguing marches. We came up with the enemy on the south [west] bank of the Shenandoah River July [18th] when we were severely repulsed & driven across the river in grate confusion. Our position was behind a fence partially made of stone and fence rails. We were laying on the ground firing. The ball that hit your husband passed between two rails entered his head just above the right eye passing mainly through the head. He died before we left the ground. Your husband and others in my own Regt was mostly a strange to me but was a good soldier and died a brave man loved and respected by his comrades.

Permit me madam to offer you my sincerest sympathies in your bereavement and let it be a consolation to know that your husband fell in a good cause facing the enemys of his country and received decent burial at our hands.

I am madam your obedient servant

G.W. Byard
Lieut 2nd Ohio Cav.

P.S. His grave is on the south [west] bank of the river about a mile below the ferry at Snickers Gap

Private Anthony W. Stumpe to Mary Wright
(Widows Pension File, National Archives and Records Administration)

Months after Pvt. William Wright, a soldier in Young's dismounted command, died at Cool Spring, Wright's widow, Mary, sought additional information about her husband's death for her claim to a widow's pension. On September 27, 1864, Pvt. Anthony W. Stumpe, one of Wright's comrades, offered some details about her husband's death and to whom she might write if she desired additional information.

Camp Stoneman
Sep. 27

Mrs. Wright:

I was asked by a Friend of your dear Husband to write to you and inform you who was in charge of our Detachment. Mr. Palmer who you wrote to was taken sick and sent to the Hospital and whether he wrote you I did not know. We were in charge of Col. Young and Major Sawyer. You would do best to write to Major Sawyer who is commanding here at present and he will give you all the particulars inquired. On the 18th day of July we crossd the Shenandoah River near Snickers Gap at 4 o'clock P.M. and Fought 3 hours. He was lying the second man from me behind a stone fence. I saw him rise to shoot when the fatal bullet took him in the head and caused his instant death. We were driven across the River and had to leave all our dead and wounded in the Rebel hands. I was very sorry for poor Wright. He was a good soldier as well as [a] good Christian and I hope he is in a better World than this. I will close my letter and give you the address required.

Yours Respectfully
A. W. Stumpe
5th U.S. Cavalry
Major Sawyer
Commanding 3 Div's.
Camp Stoneman
Washington D.C.

Today's visitors to the battlefield's peaceful fields can explore how what occurred there impacted soldiers and their families in its immediate aftermath and for decades after the Civil War's end. (jn)

Battlefield Interpretation and the Human Experience

APPENDIX G

Historians have an array of tools at their disposal to make history accessible to broader audiences, but arguably none is more significant than place. History, as Thompson Mayes, vice president and senior counsel at the National Trust for Historic Preservation, rightfully noted in his thoughtful book *Why Old Places Matter*, "is most vividly learned and retained through experiencing the places where history happened." For Civil War historians no place is more significant than the battlefield.

Like most, if not all, Civil War historians I subscribe to the notion that Civil War battlefields merit preservation because they are hallowed ground, but they are much more than that. Battlefields offer a tangible connection with the past and provide an opportunity to learn from the greatest of all teachers, history. Simply put, battlefields, as historian Gary Gallagher observed in his outstanding anthology *The Enduring Civil War*, "bring the past vividly to life" and permit visitors "to make a connection with earlier Americans that cannot be duplicated in a classroom." Gallagher's profound observation applies to all Civil War battlefields, whether one of the conflict's most significant engagements, such as Gettysburg, or one of the war's lesser-known clashes like Cool Spring.

From the moment I assumed the responsibility of managing interpretive efforts at Cool Spring in January 2017, I wanted to bring the battle to life for visitors. Typical of any battlefield interpretation, I wanted to aid visitors in comprehending

The author (left) with his graduate mentor, Dr. James I. "Bud" Robertson Jr., during a sesquicentennial event at Cross Keys in 2012. (jn)

why the battle was fought, grasping the fight's ebb and flow, and understanding how what occurred along the banks of the Shenandoah River fit into the Civil War's broader story. However, resurrecting the battle's story proved only one goal. I wanted those who visited the now peaceful landscape to come away with more than knowledge about what happened there.

Cognizant that Cool Spring attracts a multitude of visitors each year with varied interests including history, the natural environment, or self-care, not dissimilar to any other battlefield, I believed it critical to present Cool Spring's history in a way that made it relevant to all who visited. Dr. James I. "Bud" Robertson Jr., my graduate professor at Virginia Tech, incessantly reminded me that the best way to demonstrate history's applicability to people from all walks of life was to explore that history through the lens of individual human experiences. History after all was, as Robertson noted, at its core about people.

Robertson's axiom has influenced much of my professional life and has profoundly shaped the way I approach battlefield interpretation at Cool Spring. Exploring Cool Spring's history, or any battle's history through that of individuals, underscores the reality that engagements are not fought by blue and red blocks on a map, but by people of flesh and blood— humans with plans, hopes, and dreams interrupted by war. Interpretation at battlefields centered on the human experience provides a means to explore the complexities soldiers confronted, contemplate the myriad ways battle impacted soldiers and their loved ones, and explore the tragic consequences of what occurs when a people become divided to an unbridgeable point.

THE BATTLE OF COOL SPRING
(JULY 17–18, 1864)

While traditional orders of battle for the clash at Cool Spring usually only include troops engaged on July 18, this order of battle includes those units engaged the previous day at Castleman's Ferry.

UNION FORCES
Maj. Gen. Horatio G. Wright, VI Corps
Commanding Union Pursuit Force

The Army of West Virginia
Brevet Major General George Crook

First Division: Col. Joseph Thoburn

First Brigade: Col. George Wells
5th New York Heavy Artillery • 34th Massachusetts • 116th Ohio • 123rd Ohio • 170th Ohio

Second Brigade: Col. Joseph Thoburn
*1st West Virginia • 4th West Virginia • 12th West Virginia • 18th Connecticut
2nd Maryland Eastern Shore • 2nd Maryland Potomac Home Brigade*

Third Brigade (from Second Infantry Division): Col. Daniel Frost
11th West Virginia • 15th West Virginia • 54th Pennsylvania

Provisional Brigade: Lt. Col. Samuel K. Young
Dismounted cavalry from 27 different cavalry regiments

Artillery: Capt. Alexander C. Moore
1st West Virginia Light Artillery, Battery E

Batteries from VI Corps: Col. Charles H. Tompkins
*1st Rhode Island Light Artillery, Battery C • 1st Rhode Island Light Artillery, Battery G
5th U.S. Artillery, Battery L*

Cavalry
First Division: Brig. Gen. Alfred N. Duffié

First Brigade: Col. William B. Tibbits
2nd Maryland Potomac Home Brigade (detachment) • 12th Pennsylvania • 15th New York • 21st New York

Second Brigade: Lt. Col. Gabriel Middleton
1st New York Lincoln • 1st New York Veteran • 20th Pennsylvania • 22nd Pennsylvania

CONFEDERATE FORCES
Lt. Gen. Jubal A. Early
Commanding Confederate Army of the Valley District

Rodes's Division: Maj. Gen. Robert E. Rodes

Cox's Brigade: Brig. Gen. William R. Cox
*1st North Carolina • 2nd North Carolina • 3rd North Carolina • 4th North Carolina
14th North Carolina • 30th North Carolina*

Grimes's Brigade: Col. William A. Owens
*2nd North Carolina Battalion • 32nd North Carolina • 43rd North Carolina • 45th North Carolina
53rd North Carolina*

Battle's Brigade: Col. Samuel B. Pickens
3rd Alabama • 5th Alabama • 6th Alabama • 12th Alabama • 61st Alabama

Doles's Brigade: Col. Philip Cook
4th Georgia • 12th Georgia • 21st Georgia • 44th Georgia

Gordon's Division: Maj. Gen. John B. Gordon

Evans's Brigade: Col. Edmund N. Atkinson
12th Georgia Battalion • 13th Georgia • 26th Georgia • 31st Georgia • 60th Georgia • 61st Georgia

York's Brigade: Brig. Gen. Zebulon York
1st Louisiana • 2nd Louisiana • 10th Louisiana • 14th Louisiana • 15th Louisiana

Terry's Brigade: Brig. Gen. William Terry
2nd Virginia • 4th Virginia • 5th Virginia • 27th Virginia • 33rd Virginia

Jones's Brigade: Col. Robert H. Dungan
21st Virginia • 25th Virginia • 42nd Virginia • 44th Virginia • 48th Virginia • 50th Virginia

Steuart's Brigade: Lt. Col. Samuel H. Saunders
10th Virginia • 23rd Virginia • 37th Virginia Battalion

Wharton's Division: Brig. Gen. Gabriel C. Wharton

Wharton's Brigade: Lt. Col. John P. Wolfe
45th Virginia • 51st Virginia • 30th Virginia Battalion

Echols's Brigade: Col. George S. Patton
22nd Virginia • 23rd Virginia • 26th Virginia Battalion

Smith's Brigade: Col. Augustus Forsberg
36th Virginia • 60th Virginia • 45th Virginia Battalion

Artillery: Lt. Col. John Floyd King
Bryan's Lewisburg Battery • Chapman's Monroe Battery • Lowry's Wise Legion Battery

Suggested Reading

THE BATTLE OF COOL SPRING

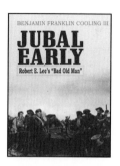

Jubal Early: Robert E. Lee's "Bad Old Man"
Benjamin Franklin Cooling III
Rowman & Littlefield, 2014
ISBN-13: 978-0810889132

Cooling's fast-paced biography of Early offers a keen
assessment of Early's life, leadership, and influence on Civil
War history. This biography is vital for anyone seeking
a deeper understanding of Early's generalship in the
Shenandoah Valley during the summer of 1864.

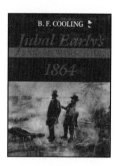

Jubal Early's Raid on Washington: 1864
Benjamin Franklin Cooling III
The Nautical & Aviation Publishing Company of America,
1989
ISBN: 093385286X

This classic study offers arguably the finest history of
Early's push to Washington's outskirts in July 1864 and
withdrawal into the Shenandoah Valley. Cooling's study
offers much insight into President Lincoln's mood in
the wake of Early's advance to the nation's capital and
Lincoln's desire to destroy Early's Army of the Valley.

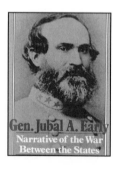

Narrative of the War Between the States
Gen. Jubal A. Early
DaCapo, 1989
ISBN: 0306804247

Originally published in 1912 as *Autobiographical Sketch and
Narrative of the War Between the States,* Early's reminiscences
provide important insight into his Confederate service.
This book is particularly valuable for those seeking Early's
perspective on operations in the Shenandoah Valley in 1864.

Shenandoah Summer: The 1864 Valley Campaign
Scott C. Patchan
University of Nebraska Press, 2007
ISBN-13: 978-0803237544

Well-written, historically balanced, and exhaustively
researched Patchan's study of operations in the Valley during
the summer of 1864 is a foundational text for anyone seeking
a deeper understanding of the conflict in the Shenandoah.

Archaeological Perspectives on the American Civil War
Clarence R. Geier and Stephen R. Potter (eds.)
University Press of Florida, 2000
ISBN: 0813026512

While this volume contains eighteen essays about a wide
array of topics, one essay in this volume is fundamental for
any student of the battle of Cool Spring: "The Battle of Cool
Spring, July 16–20, 1864" by Joseph W. A. Whitehorne and
Clarence R. Geier. This essay provides a deep analysis of the
battlefield's landscape and how it impacted the engagement.

*Worthy of a Higher Rank: The 1864 Shenandoah Valley Campaign
Journal of Colonel Joseph Thoburn, Commander First Infantry Division,
Army of West Virginia*
Scott C. Patchan (ed.)
35th Star Publishing, 2021
ISBN-13: 978-1735073996

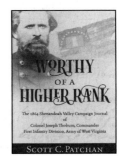

Arguably the most significant published primary source related
to the battle of Cool Spring, Thoburn's journal provides
tremendous insight into the innermost thoughts of the officer
tasked with fending off repeated Confederate assaults at the
battle of Cool Spring.

The Papers of Ulysses S. Grant: Volume 11: June 1–August 15, 1864
John Y. Simon (ed.)
Southern Illinois University Press, 1984
ISBN: 0809311178

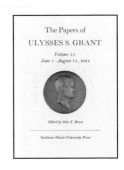

This collection of documents penned by and to Lt. Gen.
Ulysses S. Grant during the period of Early's advance toward
Washington and the Union pursuit offers an important
window into the thoughts of Union war planners as they
developed a plan to pursue Early as his Army of the Valley
withdrew to the Shenandoah Valley.

*The Civil War Journal of Mary Greenhow Lee (Mrs. Hugh Holmes Lee
of Winchester, Virginia)*
Eloise C. Strader (ed.)
Winchester-Frederick County Historical Society, 2011
ISBN: 0923198431

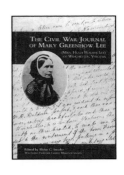

Mary Greenhow Lee's journal is essential for anyone seeking
a civilian's perspective on events. Her diary is of particular
interest to anyone interested in the aftermath of the battle of
Cool Spring as she volunteered to nurse Confederate soldiers
brought to Winchester.

About the Author

Jonathan A. Noyalas is a history professor at Shenandoah University and director of its McCormick Civil War Institute. He is the author or editor of fifteen books and has published more than 100 articles, chapters, essays, and reviews in a variety of popular and scholarly publications including *Civil War Times*, *America's Civil War*, *Civil War Monitor*, and *Civil War History*. Noyalas has appeared on NPR's "With Good Reason," PCN, and C-SPAN. Noyalas is the recipient of numerous awards for his teaching and scholarship, including Shenandoah University's Exemplary Teaching Award for the First Year Seminar, Shenandoah's Wilkins Award, and the State Council for Higher Education in Virginia's Outstanding Faculty Award.